INVISIBLE MAN

Ralph Ellison

SPARK PUBLISHING

Spark Publishing
A Division of Barnes & Noble
120 Fifth Avenue
New York, NY 10011
www.sparknotes.com

ISBN-13: 978-1-4114-0496-0
ISBN-10: 1-4114-0496-3

Please submit changes or report errors to www.sparknotes.com/errors.

Printed in the United States.

10 9 8 7 6 5 4 3 2

CONTENTS

CONTEXT

THE GRANDSON OF SLAVES, Ralph Ellison was born in 1914 in Oklahoma City, Oklahoma, and was raised largely in Tulsa, Oklahoma. His father was a construction worker, and his mother was a domestic servant who also volunteered for the local Socialist Party. As a young man, Ellison developed an abiding interest in jazz music; he befriended a group of musicians who played in a regional band called Walter Page's Blue Devils, many of whom later played with Count Basie's legendary big band in the late 1930s. Ellison himself studied the cornet and trumpet, and planned a career as a jazz musician. In 1933, he left Oklahoma to begin a study of music at the Tuskegee Institute in Tuskegee, Alabama. The Institute, which is now called Tuskegee University, was founded in 1881 by Booker T. Washington, one of the foremost black educators in American history, and became one of the nation's most important black colleges. It later served as the model for the black college attended by the narrator in *Invisible Man*.

Ellison left the Tuskegee Institute in 1936 and moved to New York City, where he settled in Harlem. As an employee of the Federal Writers' Project, Ellison befriended many of the most important African-American writers of the era, including Langston Hughes and Richard Wright. Ellison also befriended the eminent jazz writer and sociologist Albert Murray, with whom he carried on a lengthy and important literary correspondence, later collected in the book *Trading Twelves*. After a year editing the Negro Quarterly, Ellison left for the Merchant Marines, in which he served during World War II. After the war, Ellison won a Rosenwald Fellowship, which he used to write *Invisible Man*. The first chapter appeared in America in the 1948 volume of *Magazine of the Year*, and the novel was published in its entirety in 1952.

Employing a shifting, improvisational style directly based on Ellison's experience of jazz performance, *Invisible Man* ranges in tone from realism to extreme surrealism, from tragedy to vicious satire to near-slapstick comedy. Rich in symbolism and metaphor, virtuosic in its use of multiple styles and tones, and steeped in the black experience in America and the human struggle for individuality, the novel spent sixteen weeks on the best-seller list and won the

National Book Award in 1953. Achieving one of the most sensational debuts of any novel in American history, Invisible Man was hailed by writers such as Saul Bellow and critics such as Irving Howe as a landmark publication; some critics claimed that it was the most important American novel to appear after World War II.

Invisible Man was heavily influenced by the work of a number of twentieth-century French writers known as the existentialists. Existentialism, whose foremost proponents included Albert Camus and Jean-Paul Sartre, explored the question of individuality and the nature of meaning in a seemingly meaningless universe. Ellison adapted the existentialists' universal themes to the black experience of oppression and prejudice in America. He also engaged powerfully with the tradition of African-American social debate. In the character of Dr. Bledsoe, the novel offers a vehement rejection of the philosophy of Booker T. Washington, which advocated that blacks should work toward economic success as a means of achieving racial equality. It also critiques, through the character of Ras the Exhorter, Marcus Garvey's philosophy of black nationalism.

Despite—or possibly because of—the overwhelming success of Invisible Man, Ellison never published another novel in his lifetime. Though he published two books of essays—Shadow Act in the 1960s and Going to the Territory in the 1980s—Ellison spent his later decades laboring on a vast novel, which he never finished. Upon his death in 1994, Ellison left behind more than 2,000 pages of unedited, incomplete manuscript. In heavily abridged and edited form, this manuscript was published five years after his death under the title Juneteenth, to generally unfavorable reviews.

PLOT OVERVIEW

THE NARRATOR BEGINS telling his story with the claim that he is an "invisible man." His invisibility, he says, is not a physical condition—he is not literally invisible—but is rather the result of the refusal of others to see him. He says that because of his invisibility, he has been hiding from the world, living underground and stealing electricity from the Monopolated Light & Power Company. He burns 1,369 light bulbs simultaneously and listens to Louis Armstrong's "(What Did I Do to Be So) Black and Blue" on a phonograph. He says that he has gone underground in order to write the story of his life and invisibility.

As a young man, in the late 1920s or early 1930s, the narrator lived in the South. Because he is a gifted public speaker, he is invited to give a speech to a group of important white men in his town. The men reward him with a briefcase containing a scholarship to a prestigious black college, but only after humiliating him by forcing him to fight in a "battle royal" in which he is pitted against other young black men, all blindfolded, in a boxing ring. After the battle royal, the white men force the youths to scramble over an electrified rug in order to snatch at fake gold coins. The narrator has a dream that night in which he imagines that his scholarship is actually a piece of paper reading "To Whom It May Concern . . . Keep This Nigger-Boy Running."

Three years later, the narrator is a student at the college. He is asked to drive a wealthy white trustee of the college, Mr. Norton, around the campus. Norton talks incessantly about his daughter, then shows an undue interest in the narrative of Jim Trueblood, a poor, uneducated black man who impregnated his own daughter. After hearing this story, Norton needs a drink, and the narrator takes him to the Golden Day, a saloon and brothel that normally serves black men. A fight breaks out among a group of mentally imbalanced black veterans at the bar, and Norton passes out during the chaos. He is tended by one of the veterans, who claims to be a doctor and who taunts both Norton and the narrator for their blindness regarding race relations.

Back at the college, the narrator listens to a long, impassioned sermon by the Reverend Homer A. Barbee on the subject of the college's Founder, whom the blind Barbee glorifies with poetic language. After the sermon, the narrator is chastised by the college president, Dr. Bledsoe, who has learned of the narrator's misadventures with Norton at the old slave quarters and the Golden Day. Bledsoe rebukes the narrator, saying that he should have shown the white man an idealized version of black life. He expels the narrator, giving him seven letters of recommendation addressed to the college's white trustees in New York City, and sends him there in search of a job.

The narrator travels to the bright lights and bustle of 1930s Harlem, where he looks unsuccessfully for work. The letters of recommendation are of no help. At last, the narrator goes to the office of one of his letters' addressees, a trustee named Mr. Emerson. There he meets Emerson's son, who opens the letter and tells the narrator that he has been betrayed: the letters from Bledsoe actually portray the narrator as dishonorable and unreliable. The young Emerson helps the narrator to get a low-paying job at the Liberty Paints plant, whose trademark color is "Optic White." The narrator briefly serves as an assistant to Lucius Brockway, the black man who makes this white paint, but Brockway suspects him of joining in union activities and turns on him. The two men fight, neglecting the paint-making; consequently, one of the unattended tanks explodes, and the narrator is knocked unconscious.

The narrator wakes in the paint factory's hospital, having temporarily lost his memory and ability to speak. The white doctors seize the arrival of their unidentified black patient as an opportunity to conduct electric shock experiments. After the narrator recovers his memory and leaves the hospital, he collapses on the street. Some black community members take him to the home of Mary, a kind woman who lets him live with her for free in Harlem and nurtures his sense of black heritage. One day, the narrator witnesses the eviction of an elderly black couple from their Harlem apartment. Standing before the crowd of people gathered before the apartment, he gives an impassioned speech against the eviction. Brother Jack overhears his speech and offers him a position as a spokesman for the Brotherhood, a political organization that allegedly works to help the socially oppressed. After initially rejecting the offer, the narrator takes the job in order to pay Mary back for her hospitality. But the Brotherhood demands that the narrator take a new name, break with his past, and move to a new apartment. The narrator is inducted into the Brotherhood at a party at the Chthonian Hotel and is placed in charge of advancing the group's goals in Harlem.

After being trained in rhetoric by a white member of the group named Brother Hambro, the narrator goes to his assigned branch in Harlem, where he meets the handsome, intelligent black youth leader Tod Clifton. He also becomes familiar with the black nationalist leader Ras the Exhorter, who opposes the interracial Brotherhood and believes that black Americans should fight for their rights over and against all whites. The narrator delivers speeches and becomes a high-profile figure in the Brotherhood, and he enjoys his work. One day, however, he receives an anonymous note warning him to remember his place as a black man in the Brotherhood. Not long after, the black Brotherhood member Brother Wrestrum accuses the narrator of trying to use the Brotherhood to advance a selfish desire for personal distinction. While a committee of the Brotherhood investigates the charges, the organization moves the narrator to another post, as an advocate of women's rights. After giving a speech one evening, he is seduced by one of the white women at the gathering, who attempts to use him to play out her sexual fantasies about black men.

After a short time, the Brotherhood sends the narrator back to Harlem, where he discovers that Clifton has disappeared. Many other black members have left the group, as much of the Harlem community feels that the Brotherhood has betrayed their interests. The narrator finds Clifton on the street selling dancing "Sambo" dolls—dolls that invoke the stereotype of the lazy and obsequious slave. Clifton apparently does not have a permit to sell his wares on the street. White policemen accost him and, after a scuffle, shoot him dead as the narrator and others look on. On his own initiative, the narrator holds a funeral for Clifton and gives a speech in which he portrays his dead friend as a hero, galvanizing public sentiment in Clifton's favor. The Brotherhood is furious with him for staging the funeral without permission, and Jack harshly castigates him. As Jack rants about the Brotherhood's ideological stance, a glass eye falls from one of his eye sockets. The Brotherhood sends the narrator back to Brother Hambro to learn about the organization's new strategies in Harlem.

The narrator leaves feeling furious and anxious to gain revenge on Jack and the Brotherhood. He arrives in Harlem to find the neighborhood in ever-increased agitation over race relations. Ras confronts him, deploring the Brotherhood's failure to draw on the momentum generated by Clifton's funeral. Ras sends his men to beat up the narrator, and the narrator is forced to disguise himself in dark glasses and a hat. In his dark glasses, many people on the streets mistake him for someone named Rinehart, who seems to be a pimp, bookie, lover, and reverend all at once. At last, the narrator goes to Brother Hambro's apartment, where Hambro tells him that the Brotherhood has chosen not to emphasize Harlem and the black movement. He cynically declares that people are merely tools and that the larger interests of the Brotherhood are more important than any individual. Recalling advice given to him by his grandfather, the narrator determines to undermine the Brotherhood by seeming to go along with them completely. He decides to flatter and seduce a woman close to one of the party leaders in order to obtain secret information about the group.

But the woman he chooses, Sybil, knows nothing about the Brotherhood and attempts to use the narrator to fulfill her fantasy of being raped by a black man. While still with Sybil in his apartment, the narrator receives a call asking him to come to Harlem quickly. The narrator hears the sound of breaking glass, and the line goes dead. He arrives in Harlem to find the neighborhood in the midst of a full-fledged riot, which he learns was incited by Ras. The narrator becomes involved in setting fire to a tenement building. Running from the scene of the crime, he encounters Ras, dressed as an African chieftain. Ras calls for the narrator to be lynched. The narrator flees, only to encounter two policemen, who suspect that his briefcase contains loot from the riots. In his attempt to evade them, the narrator falls down a manhole. The police mock him and draw the cover over the manhole.

The narrator says that he has stayed underground ever since; the end of his story is also the beginning. He states that he finally has realized that he must honor his individual complexity and remain true to his own identity without sacrificing his responsibility to the community. He says that he finally feels ready to emerge from underground.

CHARACTER LIST

The narrator The nameless protagonist of the novel. The narrator
is the "invisible man" of the title. A black man
in 1930s America, the narrator considers himself
invisible because people never see his true self beneath
the roles that stereotype and racial prejudice compel
him to play. Though the narrator is intelligent, deeply
introspective, and highly gifted with language, the
experiences that he relates demonstrate that he
was naive in his youth. As the novel progresses, the
narrator's illusions are gradually destroyed through
his experiences as a student at college, as a worker at
the Liberty Paints plant, and as a member of a political
organization known as the Brotherhood. Shedding his
blindness, he struggles to arrive at a conception of his
identity that honors his complexity as an individual
without sacrificing social responsibility.

Brother Jack The white and blindly loyal leader of the
Brotherhood, a political organization that professes to
defend the rights of the socially oppressed. Although
he initially seems compassionate, intelligent, and
kind, and he claims to uphold the rights of the
socially oppressed, Brother Jack actually possesses
racist viewpoints and is unable to see people as
anything other than tools. His glass eye and his red
hair symbolize his blindness and his communism,
respectively.

Tod Clifton A black member of the Brotherhood and a resident
of Harlem. Tod Clifton is passionate, handsome,
articulate, and intelligent. He eventually parts ways
with the Brotherhood, though it remains unclear
whether a falling-out has taken place, or whether he
has simply become disillusioned with the group. He
begins selling Sambo dolls on the street, seemingly

both perpetrating and mocking the offensive stereotype of the lazy and servile slave that the dolls represent.

Ras the Exhorter A stout, flamboyant, charismatic, angry man with a flair for public agitation. Ras represents the black nationalist movement, which advocates the violent overthrow of white supremacy. Ellison seems to use him to comment on the black nationalist leader Marcus Garvey, who believed that blacks would never achieve freedom in white society. A maverick, Ras frequently opposes the Brotherhood and the narrator, often violently, and incites riots in Harlem.

Rinehart A surreal figure who never appears in the book except by reputation. Rinehart possesses a seemingly infinite number of identities, among them pimp, bookie, and preacher who speaks on the subject of "invisibility." When the narrator wears dark glasses in Harlem one day, many people mistake him for Rinehart. The narrator realizes that Rinehart's shape-shifting capacity represents a life of extreme freedom, complexity, and possibility. He also recognizes that this capacity fosters a cynical and manipulative inauthenticity. Rinehart thus figures crucially in the book's larger examination of the problem of identity and self-conception.

Dr. Bledsoe The president at the narrator's college. Dr. Bledsoe proves selfish, ambitious, and treacherous. He is a black man who puts on a mask of servility to the white community. Driven by his desire to maintain his status and power, he declares that he would see every black man in the country lynched before he would give up his position of authority.

Mr. Norton One of the wealthy white trustees at the narrator's college. Mr. Norton is a narcissistic man who treats the narrator as a tally on his scorecard—that is, as proof that he is liberal-minded and philanthropic. Norton's wistful remarks about his daughter add an eerie quality of longing to his fascination with the story of Jim Trueblood's incest.

Reverend Homer A. Barbee A preacher from Chicago who visits the narrator's college. Reverend Barbee's fervent praise of the Founder's "vision" strikes an inadvertently ironic note, because he himself is blind. With Barbee's first name, Ellison makes reference to the Greek poet Homer, another blind orator who praised great heroes in his epic poems. Ellison uses Barbee to satirize the college's desire to transform the Founder into a similarly mythic hero.

Jim Trueblood An uneducated black man who impregnated his own daughter and who lives on the outskirts of the narrator's college campus. The students and faculty of the college view Jim Trueblood as a disgrace to the black community. To Trueblood's surprise, however, whites have shown an increased interest in him since the story of his incest spread.

The veteran An institutionalized black man who makes bitterly insightful remarks about race relations. Claiming to be a graduate of the narrator's college, the veteran tries to expose the pitfalls of the school's ideology. His bold candor angers both the narrator and Mr. Norton—the veteran exposes their blindness and hypocrisy and points out the sinister nature of their relationship. Although society has deemed him "shell-shocked" and insane, the veteran proves to be the only character who speaks the truth in the first part of the novel.

Emerson The son of one of the wealthy white trustees (whom the text also calls Emerson) of the narrator's college. The younger Emerson reads the supposed recommendation from Dr. Bledsoe and reveals Bledsoe's treachery to the narrator. He expresses sympathy for the narrator and helps him get a job, but he remains too preoccupied with his own problems to help the narrator in any meaningful way.

Mary   A serene and motherly black woman with whom the narrator stays after learning that the Men's House has banned him. Mary treats him kindly and even lets him stay for free. She nurtures his black identity and urges him to become active in the fight for racial equality.

Sybil   A white woman whom the narrator attempts to use to find out information about the Brotherhood. Sybil instead uses the narrator to act out her fantasy of being raped by a "savage" black man.

ANALYSIS OF MAJOR CHARACTERS

THE NARRATOR

The narrator not only tells the story of *Invisible Man,* he is also its principal character. Because *Invisible Man* is a bildungsroman (a type of novel that chronicles a character's moral and psychological growth), the narrative and thematic concerns of the story revolve around the development of the narrator as an individual. Additionally, because the narrator relates the story in the first person, the text doesn't truly probe the consciousness of any other figure in the story. Ironically, though he dominates the novel, the narrator remains somewhat obscure to the reader; most notably, he never reveals his name. The names that he is given in the hospital and in the Brotherhood, the name of his college, even the state in which the college is located—these all go unidentified. The narrator remains a voice and never emerges as an external and quantifiable presence. This obscurity emphasizes his status as an "invisible man."

For much of the story, and especially in the chapters before he joins the Brotherhood, the narrator remains extremely innocent and inexperienced. He is prone to think the best of people even when he has reason not to, and he remains consistently respectful of authority. The narrator's innocence sometimes causes him to misunderstand important events in the story, often making it necessary for the reader to look past the narrator's own interpretation of events in order to see Ellison's real intentions. Ellison uses heavy irony to allow the reader to see things that the narrator misses. After the "battle royal" in Chapter 1, for instance, the narrator accepts his scholarship from the brutish white men with gladness and gratitude. Although he passes no judgment on the white men's behavior, the men's actions provide enough evidence for the reader to denounce the men as appalling racists. While the narrator can be somewhat unreliable in this regard, Ellison makes sure that the reader perceives the narrator's blindness.

Further, because the narrator supposedly writes his story as a memoir and not while it is taking place, he also comes to recognize his former blindness. As a result, just as a division exists between Ellison and the narrator, a division arises between the narrator as a narrator and the narrator as a character. Ellison renders the narrator's voice as that of a man looking back on his experiences with greater perspective, but he ensures that the reader sees into the mind of the still-innocent character. He does so by having the narrator recall how he perceived of events when they happened rather than offer commentary on these events with the benefit of hindsight.

The narrator's innocence prevents him from recognizing the truth behind others' errant behavior and leads him to try to fulfill their misguided expectations. He remains extremely vulnerable to the identity that society thrusts upon him as an African American. He plays the role of the servile black man to the white men in Chapter 1; he plays the industrious, uncomplaining disciple of Booker T. Washington during his college years; he agrees to act as the Brotherhood's black spokesperson, which allows the Brotherhood to use him. But the narrator also proves very intelligent and deeply introspective, and as a result, he is able to realize the extent to which his social roles limit him from discovering his individual identity. He gradually assumes a mask of invisibility in order to rebel against this limitation.

The narrator first dons the mask after his falling-out with the Brotherhood, in Chapter 22. He becomes even more invisible in Chapter 23, when, escaping Ras's henchmen, he disguises himself behind dark glasses and a hat, unintentionally inducing others to mistake him for the nebulous Rinehart. Finally, in Chapter 25, he retreats underground. Yet, in the act of telling his story, the narrator comes to realize the danger of invisibility: while it preempts others' attempts to define him, it also preempts his own attempts to define and express himself. He concludes his story determined to honor his own complexity rather than subdue it in the interest of a group or ideology. Though most of the narrator's difficulties arise from the fact that he is black, Ellison repeatedly emphasized his intent to render the narrator as a universal character, a representation of the struggle to define oneself against societal expectations.

BROTHER JACK

Ellison uses Brother Jack, the leader of the Brotherhood, to point out the failure of abstract ideologies to address the real plight of African Americans and other victims of oppression. At first, Jack seems kind, compassionate, intelligent, and helpful, a real boon to the struggling narrator, to whom he gives money, a job, and—seemingly—a way to help his people fight against prejudice. But as the story progresses, it becomes clear that the narrator is just as invisible to Jack as he is to everyone else. Jack sees him not as a person but as a tool for the advancement of the Brotherhood's goals. It eventually becomes clear to the narrator that Jack shares the same racial prejudices as the rest of white American society, and, when the Brotherhood's focus changes, Jack abandons the black community without regret.

The narrator's discovery that Jack has a glass eye occurs as Jack enters into a fierce tirade on the aims of the Brotherhood. His literal blindness thus symbolizes how his unwavering commitment to the Brotherhood's ideology has blinded him, metaphorically, to the plight of blacks. He tells the narrator, "We do not shape our policies to the mistaken and infantile notions of the man in the street. Our job is not to ask them what they think but to tell them!" Throughout the book, Jack explains the Brotherhood's goals in terms of an abstract ideology. He tells the narrator in Chapter 14 that the group works "for a better world for all people" and that the organization is striving to remedy the effects of too many people being "dispossessed of their heritage." He and the other brothers attempt to make the narrator's own speeches more scientific, injecting them with abstractions and jargon in order to distance them from the hard realities that the narrator seeks to expose.

To many black intellectuals in the 1930s, including Ellison, the Communist Party in particular seemed to offer the kind of salvation that Jack appears to embody—only to betray and discard the African-American cause as the party's focus shifted in the early 1940s. Ellison's treatment of the Brotherhood is largely a critique of the poor treatment that he believed the black community had received from communism, and Jack, with his red hair, seems to symbolize this betrayal.

RAS THE EXHORTER

One of the most memorable characters in the novel, Ras the Exhorter (later called Ras the Destroyer) is a powerful figure who seems to embody Ellison's fears for the future of the civil rights battle in America. Ras's name, which literally means "Prince" in one of the languages of Ethiopia, sounds simultaneously like "race" and "Ra," the Egyptian sun god. These allusions capture the essence of the character: as a passionate black nationalist, Ras is obsessed with the idea of race; as a magnificently charismatic leader, he has a kind of godlike power in the novel, even if he doesn't show a deity's wisdom. Ras's guiding philosophy, radical at the time the novel was published, states that blacks should cast off oppression and prejudice by destroying the ability of white men to control them. This philosophy leads inevitably to violence, and, as a result, both Ellison and the narrator fear and oppose such notions. Yet, although Ellison objects to the ideology that Ras embodies, he never portrays him as a clear-cut villain. Throughout the novel, the reader witnesses Ras exert a magnetic pull on crowds of black Americans in Harlem. He offers hope and courage to many. By the late 1960s, many black leaders, including Malcolm X, were advocating ideas very similar to those of Ras.

Ras, who is depicted as a West Indian, has reminded many critics of Marcus Garvey, a Jamaican-born black nationalist who was influential in the early 1920s. Like Ras, Garvey was a charismatic racial separatist with a love of flamboyant costumes who advocated black pride and argued against integration with whites. (Garvey even endorsed the Ku Klux Klan for working to keep whites and blacks separate.) However, Ellison consistently denied patterning Ras specifically on Garvey. If any link does exist, it is probably only that Garvey inspired the idea of Ras, not that Ellison attempted to recreate Garvey in Ras.

Themes, Motifs & Symbols

Themes

Themes are the fundamental and often universal ideas explored in a literary work.

Racism as an Obstacle to Individual Identity

As the narrator of *Invisible Man* struggles to arrive at a conception of his own identity, he finds his efforts complicated by the fact that he is a black man living in a racist American society. Throughout the novel, the narrator finds himself passing through a series of communities, from the Liberty Paints plant to the Brotherhood, with each microcosm endorsing a different idea of how blacks should behave in society. As the narrator attempts to define himself through the values and expectations imposed on him, he finds that, in each case, the prescribed role limits his complexity as an individual and forces him to play an inauthentic part.

Upon arriving in New York, the narrator enters the world of the Liberty Paints plant, which achieves financial success by subverting blackness in the service of a brighter white. There, the narrator finds himself involved in a process in which white depends heavily on black—both in terms of the mixing of the paint tones and in terms of the racial makeup of the workforce. Yet the factory denies this dependence in the final presentation of its product, and the narrator, as a black man, ends up stifled. Later, when the narrator joins the Brotherhood, he believes that he can fight for racial equality by working within the ideology of the organization, but he then finds that the Brotherhood seeks to use him as a token black man in its abstract project.

Ultimately, the narrator realizes that the racial prejudice of others causes them to see him only as they want to see him, and their limitations of vision in turn place limitations on his ability to act. He concludes that he is invisible, in the sense that the world is filled with blind people who cannot or will not see his real nature. Correspondingly, he remains unable to act according to his own personality and becomes literally unable to be himself. Although the narrator initially embraces his invisibility in an attempt to throw off the limiting nature of stereotype, in the end he finds this tactic too passive. He determines to emerge from his underground "hibernation," to make his own contributions to society as a complex individual. He will attempt to exert his power on the world outside of society's system of prescribed roles. By making proactive contributions to society, he will force others to acknowledge him, to acknowledge the existence of beliefs and behaviors outside of their prejudiced expectations.

THE LIMITATIONS OF IDEOLOGY

Over the course of the novel, the narrator realizes that the complexity of his inner self is limited not only by people's racism but also by their more general ideologies. He finds that the ideologies advanced by institutions prove too simplistic and one-dimensional to serve something as complex and multidimensional as human identity. The novel contains many examples of ideology, from the tamer, ingratiating ideology of Booker T. Washington subscribed to at the narrator's college to the more violent, separatist ideology voiced by Ras the Exhorter. But the text makes its point most strongly in its discussion of the Brotherhood. Among the Brotherhood, the narrator is taught an ideology that promises to save "the people," though, in reality, it consistently limits and betrays the freedom of the individual. The novel implies that life is too rich, too various, and too unpredictable to be bound up neatly in an ideology; like jazz, of which the narrator is particularly fond, life reaches the heights of its beauty during moments of improvisation and surprise.

THE DANGER OF FIGHTING STEREOTYPE WITH STEREOTYPE

The narrator is not the only African American in the book to have felt the limitations of racist stereotyping. While he tries to escape the grip of prejudice on an individual level, he encounters other blacks who attempt to prescribe a defense strategy for all African Americans. Each presents a theory of the supposed right way to be black in America and tries to outline how blacks should act in accordance with this theory. The espousers of these theories believe that anyone who acts contrary to their prescriptions effectively betrays the race. Ultimately, however, the narrator finds that such prescriptions only counter stereotype with stereotype and replace one limiting role with another.

Early in the novel, the narrator's grandfather explains his belief that in order to undermine and mock racism, blacks should exaggerate their servility to whites. The narrator's college, repre-sented by Dr. Bledsoe, thinks that blacks can best achieve success by working industriously and adopting the manners and speech of whites. Ras the Exhorter thinks that blacks should rise up and take their freedom by destroying whites. Although all of these concep-tions arise from within the black community itself, the novel implies that they ultimately prove as dangerous as white people's racist ste-reotypes. By seeking to define their identity within a race in too lim-ited a way, black figures such as Bledsoe and Ras aim to empower themselves but ultimately undermine themselves. Instead of explor-ing their own identities, as the narrator struggles to do throughout the book, Bledsoe and Ras consign themselves and their people to formulaic roles. These men consider treacherous anyone who at-tempts to act outside their formulae of blackness. But as blacks who seek to restrict and choreograph the behavior of the black American community as a whole, it is men like these who most profoundly betray their people.

MOTIFS

Motifs are recurring structures, contrasts, and literary devices that can help to develop and inform the text's major themes.

BLINDNESS

Probably the most important motif in *Invisible Man* is that of blind-ness, which recurs throughout the novel and generally represents how people willfully avoid seeing and confronting the truth. The narrator repeatedly notes that people's inability to see what they wish not to see—their inability to see that which their prejudice doesn't allow them to see—has forced him into a life of effective invisibility. But prejudice against others is not the only kind of blind-ness in the book. Many figures also refuse to acknowledge truths about themselves or their communities, and this refusal emerges consistently in the imagery of blindness. Thus, the boys who fight in the "battle royal" wear blindfolds, symbolizing their powerless-ness to recognize their exploitation at the hands of the white men. The Founder's statue at the college has empty eyes, signifying his ideology's stubborn neglect of racist realities. Blindness also afflicts Reverend Homer A. Barbee, who romanticizes the Founder, and Brother Jack, who is revealed to lack an eye—a lack that he has dis-simulated by wearing a glass eye. The narrator himself experiences moments of blindness, such as in Chapter 16 when he addresses the black community under enormous, blinding lights. In each case, failure of sight corresponds to a lack of insight.

INVISIBILITY

Because he has decided that the world is full of blind men and sleepwalkers who cannot see him for what he is, the narrator describes himself as an "invisible man." The motif of invisibility pervades the novel, often manifesting itself hand in hand with the motif of blindness—one person becomes invisible because another is blind. While the novel almost always portrays blindness in a negative light, it treats invisibility much more ambiguously. Invisibility can bring disempowerment, but it can also bring freedom and mobility. Indeed, it is the freedom the narrator derives from his anonymity that enables him to tell his story. Moreover, both the veteran at the Golden Day and the narrator's grandfather seem to endorse invisibility as a position from which one may safely exert power over others, or at least undermine others' power, without being caught. The narrator demonstrates this power in the Prologue, when he literally draws upon electrical power from his hiding place underground; the electric company is aware of its losses but cannot locate their source. At the end of the novel, however, the narrator has decided that while invisibility may bring safety, actions undertaken in secrecy cannot ultimately have any meaningful impact. One may undermine one's enemies from a position of invisibility, but one cannot make significant changes to the world. Accordingly, in the Epilogue the narrator decides to emerge from his hibernation, resolved to face society and make a visible difference.

SYMBOLS

Symbols are objects, characters, figures, and colors used to represent abstract ideas or concepts.

THE SAMBO DOLL AND THE COIN BANK

The coin bank in the shape of the grinning black man (Chapter 15) and Tod Clifton's dancing Sambo doll (Chapter 20) serve similar purposes in the novel, each representing degrading black stereotypes and the damaging power of prejudice. The coin bank, which portrays a grinning slave who eats coins, embodies the idea of the good slave who fawns over white men for trivial rewards. This stereotype literally follows the narrator, for even after he has smashed the bank and attempted to discard the pieces, various characters return to him the paper in which the pieces are wrapped. Additionally, the statue's hasty swallowing of coins mirrors the behavior of the black youths in the "battle royal" of Chapter 1, as they scramble to collect the coins on the electrified carpet, reinforcing the white stereotype of blacks as servile and humble.

The Sambo doll is made in the image of the Sambo slave, who, according to white stereotype, acts lazy yet obsequious. Moreover, as a dancing doll, it represents the negative stereotype of the black entertainer who laughs and sings for whites. While the coin bank illustrates the power of stereotype to follow a person in his or her every movement, the Sambo doll illustrates stereotype's power to control a person's movements altogether. Stereotype and prejudice, like the invisible strings by which the doll is made to move, often determine and manipulate the range of action of which a person is capable.

THE LIBERTY PAINTS PLANT

The Liberty Paints plant serves as a complex metaphor for American society with regard to race. Like America, it defines itself with notions of liberty and freedom but incorporates a deeply ingrained racism in its most central operations. By portraying a factory that produces paint, Ellison is able to make his statements about color literal. Thus, when the factory authorities boast of the superiority of their white paint, their statements appear as parodies of arguments about white supremacy. With the plant's claim that its trademark "Optic White" can cover up any tint or stain, Ellison makes a pointed observation about American society's intentions to cover up black identity with white culture, to ignore difference, and to treat darker-skinned individuals as "stains" upon white "purity."

Optic White is made through a process that involves the mixture of a number of dark-colored chemicals, one of which appears "dead black." Yet the dark colors disappear into the swirling mixture, and the paint emerges a gleaming white, showing no trace of its true components. The labor relations within the plant manifest a similar pattern: black workers perform all of the crucial labor, but white people sell the paint and make the highest wages, never acknowledging their reliance upon their darker-skinned counterparts. This dynamic, too, seems to mirror a larger one at work within America as a whole.

SUMMARY & ANALYSIS

PROLOGUE

SUMMARY
The narrator introduces himself as an "invisible man." He explains that his invisibility owes not to some biochemical accident or supernatural cause but rather to the unwillingness of other people to notice him, as he is black. It is as though other people are sleepwalkers moving through a dream in which he doesn't appear. The narrator says that his invisibility can serve both as an advantage and as a constant aggravation. Being invisible sometimes makes him doubt whether he really exists. He describes his anguished, aching need to make others recognize him, and says he has found that such attempts rarely succeed.

The narrator relates an incident in which he accidentally bumped into a tall, blond man in the dark. The blond man called him an insulting name, and the narrator attacked him, demanding an apology. He threw the blond man to the ground, kicked him, and pulled out his knife, prepared to slit the man's throat. Only at the last minute did he come to his senses. He realized that the blond man insulted him because he couldn't really see him. The next day, the narrator reads about the incident in the newspaper, only to find the attack described as a mugging. The narrator remarks upon the irony of being mugged by an invisible man.

The narrator describes the current battle that he is waging against the Monopolated Light & Power Company. He secretly lives for free in a shut-off section of a basement, in a building that allows only white tenants. He steals electricity from the company to light his room, which he has lined with 1,369 bulbs. The company knows that someone is stealing electricity from them but is unaware of the culprit's identity or location.

The narrator stays in his secret, underground home, listening to Louis Armstrong's jazz records at top volume on his phonograph. He states that he wishes that he had five record players with which to listen to Armstrong, as he likes feeling the vibrations of the music as well as hearing it. While listening, he imagines a scene in a black church and hears the voice of a black woman speaking out of the congregation. She confesses that she loved her white master because he gave her sons. Through her sons she learned to love her master, though she also hated him, for he promised to set the children free but never did. In the end, she says, she killed him with poison, knowing that her sons planned to tear him to pieces with their homemade knives. The narrator interrogates her about the idea of freedom until one of the woman's sons throws the narrator out on the street. The narrator then describes his experiences of listening to Armstrong's music under the influence of marijuana and says that the power of Armstrong's music, like the power of marijuana, comes from its ability to change one's sense of time. But eventually, the narrator notes, he stopped smoking marijuana, because he felt that it dampened his ability to take action, whereas the music to which he listened impelled him to act.

Now, the narrator hibernates in his invisibility with his invisible music, preparing for his unnamed action. He states that the beginning of his story is really the end. He asks who was responsible for his near-murder of the blond man—after all, the blond man insulted him. Though he may have been lost in a dream world of sleepwalkers, the blond man ultimately controlled the dream. Nevertheless, if the blond man had called a police officer, the narrator would have been blamed for the incident.

Analysis

The Prologue of *Invisible Man* introduces the major themes that define the rest of the novel. The metaphors of invisibility and blindness allow for an examination of the effects of racism on the victim and the perpetrator. Because the narrator is black, whites refuse to see him as an actual, three-dimensional person; hence, he portrays himself as invisible and describes them as blind.

The Prologue also helps to place the novel within larger literary and philosophical contexts. Especially apparent is the influence of existentialism, a philosophy that originated in France in the mid-twentieth century, which sought to define the meaning of individual existence in a seemingly meaningless universe. At the time of *Invisible Man*'s publication in 1952, existentialism had reached the height of its popularity; Ellison's book proposes to undertake a similar examination of the meaning of individual existence, but through the lens of race relations in postwar America. In French existentialist works, physical infirmities (such as nausea in the work of Jean-Paul Sartre and disease in the work of Albert Camus) frequently

symbolize internal struggles; Ellison locates the tension of race relations in similar conditions: invisibility and blindness.

The narrator's central struggle involves the conflict between how
others perceive him and how he perceives himself. Racist attitudes
cause others to view him in terms of racial stereotypes—as a mug-
ger, bumpkin, or savage. But the narrator desires recognition of his
individuality rather than recognition based on these stereotypes.
The "blindness" of others stems from an inability to see the narrator without imposing these alien identities on him. The narrator
notes that, given this situation, it does not matter how he thinks of
himself, because anyone—even the anonymous blond man on the
street—can force him to confront or assume an alien identity, simply by uttering a racial insult. Thus confined, the narrator flees the
outside world in search of the freedom to define himself without the
constraints that racism imposes.

The episode with the blond man and its subsequent treatment in
the newspaper serve to illustrate the extent of the narrator's metaphorical slavery. The man's insult, which we can assume was a de-
rogatory racial epithet, dehumanizes the narrator, who attacks the
man in order to force him to recognize the narrator's individuality.
The newspaper's labeling of the incident as a mugging marshals the
narrator's act of resistance against racism into the service of racism:
the blond man becomes the victim rather than the assailant, while
the narrator and his motives become invisible to the public. Others
have again managed to define the narrator's identity according to
their own prejudices.

The narrator also uses his invisibility to his advantage, however;
he can exert a force on the world without being seen, without suf-
fering the consequences. The narrator speaks to us through his written text without revealing his name, shrouding himself in another
form of invisibility in order to gain the freedom to speak freely.
We find ourselves confronted by a disembodied voice rising from
underground, the voice of one whose identity or origin remains a
secret. Invisibility also affords the narrator the opportunity to steal
electricity from the power company. By illegally draining their resources—both electrical and otherwise—he forces the company to
acknowledge his existence yet preempts any response from them,
including any racist response. By remaining metaphorically and
literally invisible to them, he announces himself as a presence but
nonetheless escapes the company's control.

The excessive lighting of the narrator's underground hole (he uses 1,369 bulbs) not only emphasizes the narrator's presence to the electric company authorities; the narrator also attempts, with this light, to "see" himself clearly without the clouding influence of outside opinion. Notably, 1,369 is the square of thirty-seven—Ellison's age at the time of writing—which ties the narrator's experience to Ellison's own sense of self.

Stylistically, Ellison's Prologue makes use of a great deal of ambiguity, both emotional and moral. The former slave woman whom the narrator encounters in his jazz daydream has mixed feelings toward her former master, loving him as the father of her sons but hating him for enslaving her and her children. Other ambiguities arise around the question of betrayal: one wonders whether the slave woman betrayed her master by poisoning him or whether she saved him from a worse fate at the hands of her sons. One may even ask whether the woman saved her sons by preventing them from becoming murderers or betrayed them by robbing them of their revenge. Similar questions arise regarding guilt in the narrator's own act of violence against the blond man. Such inquiries come to the forefront as Ellison examines the question of moral responsibility in a racist society. Ellison asks how a woman can owe love or gratitude to a man who considered her a piece of property, devoid of any emotional life. Similarly, he questions how the narrator can have any responsibility to a society that refuses to acknowledge his existence.

Ellison works blues and jazz—specifically that of Louis Armstrong—into the novel to complement the narrator's quest to define himself. Because jazz depends on the improvisational talents of individual soloists and because it developed primarily among African-American musicians, it serves as an elegant and apt metaphor for the black struggle for individuality in American society. It also makes an appropriate soundtrack, as it were, for a novel about the search for such individuality. Armstrong, widely considered the most important soloist in the history of jazz, almost single-handedly transformed jazz—which originally evolved as a collective, ensemble-based music—into a medium for individual expression in which a soloist stood out from a larger band.

In the Prologue, the narrator listens specifically to Armstrong's "(What Did I Do to Be So) Black and Blue." This track relates directly to *Invisible Man* on a thematic level, as it represents one of jazz's earliest attempts to make an open commentary on the subject of racism. Fats Waller originally wrote the song for a musical comedy in which a dark-skinned black woman would sing it as a lament, ruing her lighter-skinned lover's loss of interest in her. Later, however, Armstrong transformed the piece into a direct commentary on the hardships faced by blacks in a racist white society. Like *Invisible Man*, the song's lyrics emphasize the conflict between the singer/speaker's inner feelings and the outer identity imposed on him by society. The narrator listens to Armstrong sing that he feels "white inside" and that "my only sin / is in my skin." By placing this song in the background of his story without directly commenting on it, Ellison provides subtle reinforcement for the novel's central tension between white racism against blacks and the black struggle for individuality.

CHAPTER 1

SUMMARY

The narrator speaks of his grandparents, freed slaves who, after the Civil War, believed that they were separate but equal—that they had achieved equality with whites despite segregation. The narrator's grandfather lived a meek and quiet life after being freed. On his deathbed, however, he spoke bitterly to the narrator's father, comparing the lives of black Americans to warfare and noting that he himself felt like a traitor. He counseled the narrator's father to undermine the whites with "yeses" and "grins" and advised his family to "agree 'em to death and destruction." Now the narrator too lives meekly; he too receives praise from the white members of his town. His grandfather's words haunt him, for the old man deemed such meekness to be treachery.

The narrator recalls delivering the class speech at his high school graduation. The speech urges humility and submission as key to the advancement of black Americans. It proves such a success that the town arranges to have him deliver it at a gathering of the community's leading white citizens. The narrator arrives and receives instructions to take part in the "battle royal" that figures as part of the evening's entertainment. The narrator and some of his classmates (who are black) don boxing gloves and enter the ring. A naked, blonde, white woman with an American flag painted on her stomach parades about; some of the white men demand that the black boys look at her and others threaten them if they don't.

The white men then blindfold the youths and order them to pummel one another viciously. The narrator suffers defeat in the last round. After the men have removed the blindfolds, they lead the contestants to a rug covered with coins and a few crumpled bills. The boys lunge for the money, only to discover that an electric current runs through the rug. During the mad scramble, the white men attempt to force the boys to fall face forward onto the rug.

When it comes time for the narrator to give his speech, the white men all laugh and ignore him as he quotes, verbatim, large sections of Booker T. Washington's Atlanta Exposition Address. Amid the amused, drunken requests that he repeat the phrase "social responsibility," the narrator accidentally says "social equality." The white men angrily demand that he explain himself. He responds that he made a mistake, and finishes his speech to uproarious applause. The men award him a calfskin briefcase and instruct him to cherish it, telling him that one day its contents will help determine the fate of his people. Inside, to his utter joy, the narrator finds a scholarship to the state college for black youth. His happiness doesn't diminish when he later discovers that the gold coins from the electrified rug are actually worthless brass tokens.

That night, the narrator has a dream of going to a circus with his grandfather, who refuses to laugh at the clowns. His grandfather instructs him to open the briefcase. Inside the narrator finds an official envelope with a state seal. He opens it only to find another envelope, itself containing another envelope. The last one contains an engraved document reading: "To Whom It May Concern . . . Keep This Nigger-Boy Running." The narrator wakes with his grandfather's laughter ringing in his ears.

ANALYSIS

The narrator's grandfather introduces a further element of moral and emotional ambiguity to the novel, contributing to the mode of questioning that dominates it. While the grandfather confesses that he deems himself a traitor for his policy of meekness in the face of the South's enduring racist structure, the reader never learns whom the grandfather feels he has betrayed: himself, his family, his ancestors, future generations, or perhaps his race as a whole. While this moral ambiguity arises from the grandfather's refusal to elaborate, another ambiguity arises out of his direct instructions. For in the interest of his family's self-protection, he advises them to maintain two identities: on the outside they should embody the stereotypical good slaves, behaving just as their former masters wish; on the inside, however, they should retain their bitterness and resentment against this imposed false identity. By following this model, the grandfather's descendants can refuse internally to accept second-class status, protect their own self-respect, and avoid betraying themselves or each other.

The use of masks or role-playing as a method of subterfuge becomes increasingly important later in the novel. As others aggressively attack the individual's sense of self, the mask becomes a form of defense. Moreover, role-playing can become a kind of pointed performance art: the grandfather instructs his family members to play the role of the good slave to the extent that the role becomes almost a parody. In this way, excessive obedience to Southern whites' expectations becomes insidious disobedience: the family can "overcome [the white people] with yeses, undermine [them] with grins." The family can play upon the rift between how others perceive them and how they perceive themselves, exploiting it to their advantage.

Despite his grandfather's warnings, the narrator believes that genuine obedience will win him respect and praise. To some extent he is right, as the white men reward his obedience with a scholarship. Yet they also take advantage of his passivity, forcing him to take part in the degrading and barbaric battle royal. In addition to accentuating this tension between obedience and rebellion under the guise of obedience, the battle royal episode extends the novel's motifs of blindness and masks. The boys' literal blindfolding in the ring parallels the men's metaphorical blindness as they watch the fight: the men view the boys not as individuals, but as inferior beings, as animals. The blindfolds also represent the boys' own metaphorical blindness—their inability to see through the false masks of goodwill that barely conceal the men's racist motives as they force the boys to conform to the racial stereotype of the black man as a violent, savage, oversexed beast. The narrator, blind in so many ways, has not yet learned to see behind the masks, behind the surfaces of things, behind the veils put up by white society. Only too late does he discover the falsity of the supposedly gold coins and of white generosity—the painful electric current running through the innocuous-looking rug.

Ellison does not limit himself to symbolic language and allegorical references, however. In his presentation of the narrator's speech, Ellison directly enters into another tradition, that of black social debate. By placing this speech within the context of the events in

this chapter, he critiques and questions its stated beliefs. Specifically, he disparages the optimistic social program of the nineteenth-
century black educator and writer Booker T. Washington. Although
the narrator never actually names Washington directly, his speech
contains long quotations from the great reformer's Atlanta Exposition Address of 1895. Washington's program for the advancement
of black Americans emphasized industrial education. He believed
that blacks should avoid clamoring for political and civil rights and
put their energy instead toward achieving economic success. He believed that if blacks worked hard and proved themselves, whites
would grant them equality.

Ellison faulted this philosophy for its vastly optimistic assess-
ment of white society. The successful black businessman, after all,
proved as vulnerable to racial prejudice as the poor, uneducated
sharecropper. Ellison makes his argument by showing what happens to blacks who follow Washington's ideology, such as the narrator's grandfather, who came to believe late in his life that such
an ideology contained major limitations. Ellison's point is made
more dramatic when the white audience taunts and humiliates the
hardworking, polite narrator while he voices sections of Washington's speech. Ellison forcefully implies that racist whites are not
prepared to accept either Washington's ideas or industrious, up-
standing black citizens.

The white men's reaction to the narrator's slip in substituting
"social equality" for "social responsibility" in his speech underlines
Ellison's point. Whereas the men act with some benevolence toward
the narrator when he embodies their idea of the model black citizen,
they show their true faces when he threatens white supremacy. This
sudden hostility reveals the limitations of Washington's philosophy:
the narrator's blind obedience to the good slave role doesn't free him
from racism; rather, the moment he exhibits an individual opinion,
the men demand that he reassume the good slave role. By rewarding
him with the briefcase and scholarship only when he does so, the
men restrict his social advancement to their terms.

The men's instruction to the narrator to consider the briefcase
a "badge of office" is ironic, in that such a badge normally constitutes an insignia or emblem denoting a person's job, position, or
membership in a group ("office" here means an assigned function
or duty). The text suggests, however, that the only "office" that
the narrator has assumed is that of the good slave, an "office" that
the white men have forced upon him. The briefcase appears several

times throughout the novel as a reminder of this bitter irony of advancement through self-effacement. Although the narrator's dream hints at his vague awareness of the gift's real meaning, he is not yet conscious of its insidious nature.

As the narrator matures, however, he will develop new conceptions of race relations and come to new understandings of how to assert his own identity within and against these relations. In portraying this evolution, *Invisible Man* enters into the tradition of the bildungsroman (a German word meaning "novel of formation"), a genre of fiction that portrays a young person's education and early experience and shows the moral and intellectual growth that transforms him or her into an adult. The bildungsroman enjoyed particular popularity in eighteenth- and nineteenth-century European fiction, most notably in the works of Johann Wolfgang von Goethe (*The Sorrows of Young Werther*), Charles Dickens (*Great Expectations, David Copperfield*), and Charlotte Brontë (*Jane Eyre*). In American fiction, great examples of the bildungsroman include Mark Twain's *Huckleberry Finn* and F. Scott Fitzgerald's *This Side of Paradise*. Ellison's novel, in also addressing questions about race, individuality, and the meaning of existence, differentiates itself somewhat from the traditional "novel of formation." One might best consider it a kind of existential bildungsroman, combining the story of a young man's progress in the world with an anguished and far-reaching exploration of race, society, and identity.

CHAPTERS 2–3

SUMMARY: CHAPTER 2

Recalling his time at the college, the narrator remembers with particular fascination the college's bronze statue of its Founder, a black man. He describes the statue as cold and paternal, its eyes empty. At the end of his junior year, the narrator takes a job driving Mr. Norton, one of the college's white millionaire founders, around the campus. In an attempt to show the old gentleman the countryside near the campus, the narrator unwittingly drives Norton to an area of ramshackle cabins. The cabins, which once served as slave quarters, now house poor black sharecroppers. Though Norton finds the cabins intriguing, the narrator immediately regrets having driven him to this area, as he knows that Jim Trueblood lives here. The college regards Trueblood with hatred and distrust because he has impregnated his own daughter. Norton reacts with horror when the narrator reveals this information, but he insists on speaking with Trueblood.

Trueblood explains that he had a strange dream and woke to find himself having sex with his daughter. Norton listens with a morbid, voyeuristic fascination. Trueblood expresses wonder at the fact that white people have showered him with more money and help than before he committed the unspeakable taboo of incest. Norton, shocked at the story, hands Trueblood a one-hundred-dollar bill to buy toys for his children. He gets back into the car in a daze and requests some whiskey to calm his nerves.

SUMMARY: CHAPTER 3

The narrator, fearing that Norton might die from shock, drives to the nearest tavern, the Golden Day, which serves black people and also happens to be a brothel. As he approaches the Golden Day, the narrator encounters a group of mentally disturbed black war veterans who are being allowed an afternoon outside their home. Their attendant is nowhere to be seen. The narrator intends to dash in and out of the tavern, as the establishment has a bad reputation, but the proprietor refuses to sell take-out whiskey. Some of the veterans help carry Norton inside, since he has fallen unconscious. As they soon as they pour some whiskey down his throat, he begins to regain consciousness. The brutish attendant in charge of the veterans now appears, shouting down from the area of the building devoted to the brothel. Clad only in shorts, he asks why the veterans are yelling. A brawl ensues. Norton falls unconscious again, and the narrator and one of the veterans carry him upstairs to where the prostitutes stay.

This particular veteran claims to be a doctor and a graduate of the college. After Norton wakes, the veteran mocks Norton's interest in the narrator and the college. He says that Norton views the narrator as a mark on his scorecard of achievement rather than as a man and that the narrator thinks of Norton not as a man but as a god. He calls the narrator an automaton stricken with a blindness that makes him do Norton's bidding and claims that this blindness is the narrator's chief asset. Norton becomes angry and demands that the narrator take him back to the college. During the ride back, Norton remains completely silent.

ANALYSIS: CHAPTERS 2–3

With Ellison's first detailed image of Chapter 2, he extends his critique of the ideas upheld by Booker T. Washington and his followers. The statue honoring the Founder seems to depict an abstract father symbol rather than an actual individual. Though the Founder has allegedly made a great mark on history, we never even learn his name. His individuality and humanity seem lost in the statue's cold bronze and stiff expression. The Founder's anonymity echoes the absence of Booker T. Washington's name in the narrator's graduation speech after the "battle royal" in Chapter 1, an absence made conspicuous by the narrator's verbatim quotes from Washington's Atlanta Exposition Address. Ellison uses the Founder as a double for Washington. Both men seemingly set out to design a program for the advancement of black Americans (Washington founded the school now called Tuskegee University), and both, hailed as great visionaries, enjoy fervent worship on the part of their followers. Sadly, within the text both have become invisible men: not even a record of their names exists in the novel. By omitting their names, Ellison attempts to signify such figures' metaphoric invisibility within the real world—the futility of their actions, their failure to exert any real force on society. The novel also suggests that both men suffer blindness: with the statue's "empty" eyes, Ellison implies that Washington's philosophy is illusionary.

Part of Ellison's derision of Washington lies in his belief that Washington underestimated the power of prejudice among white Americans. Yet, in this chapter, Ellison also explores prejudice from a new angle, examining the social prejudice that emerges from economic and educational inequalities and that can exist between educated and uneducated blacks. Just as the monetary rewards of the battle royal incite the narrator and his classmates to turn on one another in Chapter 1, the rewards of social advancement offered by the college incite the students and faculty to turn their backs on one of the least-empowered groups of American blacks: the poor sharecroppers. In an attempt to conform to the role of the model black citizen expected of them by white trustees, these higher-status blacks disown the dishonorable Jim Trueblood. This attempt to break from the lower-status blacks in order to gain greater favor with the white community seems to illustrate the narrator's grandfather's statement in Chapter 1 that blind conformity to the good slave role constitutes an act of treachery.

With the character of Mr. Norton, the novel introduces another instance of white condescension and self-aggrandizement masquerading as generosity and philanthropy. Norton's interest in the college stems more from self-interest than more a genuine desire to improve the difficulties of black Americans. Explaining to the narrator why he became involved in the college, he says, in the Golden Day, "I felt . . . that your people were somehow closely connected with my destiny" (Chapter 3). Earlier, in the car, he tells the narrator, "You are my fate" (Chapter 2). Norton never concedes to the narrator the right to claim his fate as his own; instead, their fates become one, with Norton claiming ownership over both. This seemingly benevolent white man actually possesses a latent racism, and he takes pride in his work with the college because it has allowed him to direct and control human life. Although he states that the students constitute his fate and that it is his destiny to improve their lives, Norton has, in reality, put himself in the position of determining their common fate.

Norton's influence over the lives of the black students remains an insidious one; he exerts power over them while appearing to empower them. This element of deception and illusion reintroduces Ellison's motif of invisibility and blindness. Norton exerts his power invisibly, without appearing to be a controlling force; indeed, his power allows him to become intimately involved in the lives of thousands of students who have never even seen him. There is a chilling undertone to his remark to the narrator that "[y]ou are bound to a great dream and to a beautiful monument" (Chapter 2). The narrator believes that the school offers him freedom, but, in fact, he remains tied to the dreams and monuments of men like Norton—the word "bound" even invokes the image of a shackled slave. The narrator's residence and study at the college become a kind of imprisonment to which both Norton and the narrator are blind.

Norton's act of generosity to Trueblood contains the same tensions between kindness and self-interest. He takes a distinct voyeuristic delight in Trueblood's story, seeming to derive from it both entertainment and the thrill of forbidden pleasure. Indeed, Norton's detailed descriptions of his own daughter suggest that Trueblood's story may provide him with an imaginative outlet in which he vicariously can live out his own incestuous desires. Norton, who continually mentions his daughter's beauty and purity, at one point remarks,

"I could never believe her to be my own flesh and blood." The one hundred dollars that Norton gives Trueblood, then, seems a payment for describing the very sin that Norton himself seems to have wanted to commit. Although he claims that he intends the money for Trueblood's children, the gift seems tainted, like Norton's gifts to the college, by illegitimate motives, and serves to degrade rather than to help the recipient.

When the doctor-veteran at the Golden Day tavern calls the narrator an "automaton," the comment revives the problematic relationship between white benefactor and black beneficiary. The veteran explicitly identifies Norton's narcissism by stating that Norton sees the narrator as a mark on the scorecard of his achievement. "Poor stumblers," he says, "neither of you can see the other. . . ." But neither Norton nor the narrator takes kindly to having his figurative blindfold removed: just as Norton wishes to believe himself an influential humanitarian, so does the narrator wish to continue under the illusion that the college offers him the freedom to determine his own fate and identity. Ellison imbues this scene with an extremely ironic social critique: though the veteran emerges as the only character to recognize and speak the truth, society labels him insane for daring to see beneath the surface and for telling the tale of what he has seen.

CHAPTERS 4–6

SUMMARY: CHAPTER 4

Mr. Norton asks to be taken to his room and requests a personal visit from Dr. Bledsoe, the president of the college. Bledsoe becomes furious when the narrator informs him of the afternoon's events, scolding him that he should have known to show powerful white trustees only what the college wants them to see. When Bledsoe arrives at Norton's room, he orders the narrator to leave and instructs him to attend the chapel service that evening. In his room later that afternoon, the narrator receives a message that Bledsoe wants to speak with him in Norton's room. He arrives to find only Mr. Norton, however, who informs him that Bledsoe had to leave suddenly but that the narrator can find him in his office after the evening service. Norton says that he explained to Bledsoe that the narrator was not responsible for what happened and adds that he thinks that Bledsoe understands.

SUMMARY: CHAPTER 5

Reverend Homer A. Barbee speaks at the chapel service. He is African American and wears dark glasses. He tells the story of the Founder, a former slave born into poverty with a precocious intelligence. The Founder was almost killed as a child when a cousin splashed him with lye, rendering him impotent. After nine days in a coma, he woke, as if resurrected. He taught himself how to read and later escaped slavery. He went north and pursued further education. After many years, he returned to the South and founded the college to which he devoted the rest of his life's work. The sermon deeply moves the narrator. Barbee stumbles on the way back to his chair, and his glasses fall from his face. The narrator catches a glimpse of Barbee's sightless eyes and realizes that Barbee is blind.

SUMMARY: CHAPTER 6

> "I's big and black and I say 'Yes, suh' as loudly as any
> burrhead when it's convenient, but I'm still the king
> down here...."
>
> *(See* QUOTATIONS, *p. 69)*

After the service, the narrator meets with Bledsoe, who is angry that the narrator took Norton to the old slave quarters, Jim Trueblood's cabin, and the Golden Day. The narrator protests that Norton ordered him to stop at the cabin. Bledsoe replies that white people constantly give foolish orders and that the narrator, having grown up in the South as a black man, should know how to lie his way out of such situations. Bledsoe says that he will have to investigate the veteran who mocked Norton. He picks up a slave's leg shackle and informs the narrator that he must be disciplined. The narrator threatens to tell everyone that Bledsoe broke his promise to Norton not to punish him. Bledsoe responds angrily that he has worked hard to achieve his position of power and that he doesn't plan to lose it. Rather than expel the narrator outright, Bledsoe tells him to go to New York for the summer and work to earn his year's tuition. Bledsoe hints that if he does well he will earn the right to return to school. He offers to send letters of recommendation to some of the trustees to ensure that the narrator gets work. The next day, the narrator retrieves seven sealed letters and assures Bledsoe that he doesn't resent his punishment. Bledsoe praises his attitude, but the narrator remains haunted by his grandfather's prophetic dying words.

ANALYSIS: CHAPTERS 4–6

Dr. Bledsoe proves a master of masks. Imperious and commanding with the narrator, he becomes conciliatory and servile with Mr. Norton. Moreover, when the narrator protests that he drove Norton to the old slave quarters only according to orders, Bledsoe bursts out, "Damn what he wants. We take these white folks where we want them to go, we show them what we want them to see." The narrator learns, to his shock, that the surface appearance of humble servility in fact constitutes a mere mask under which Bledsoe manipulates and deceives powerful white donors to his advantage.

In this duplicity, the narrator recognizes his grandfather's sentiment that true treachery lies in believing in the mask of meekness. For, echoing Booker T. Washington's philosophy, Bledsoe practices humility and preaches the virtue of humble contentment with one's place; but, in fact, he uses his seeming passivity to mask his true aims. Bledsoe employs this mask of meekness not only as a method of self-preservation or even self-empowerment but also as a method of actively grabbing power. He uses the college and Washington's ideology to gain a position of power rather than to achieve broad social progress for his people. Bledsoe's declaration that he has "played the nigger" long and hard to get to his position and won't have one young, naive student vanquish his accomplishments reveals his priorities: his concern for the college's image masks his greater fear that his own image will be defiled and his power stripped.

To remain in power, Bledsoe must prevent the narrator from lifting his mask and exposing his duplicity. By shipping the narrator off to New York, he preserves his cover. Moreover, the proposition to get the narrator hired in New York, it soon becomes clear, constitutes an act of duplicity in itself. Though Bledsoe has no intention of helping the narrator, the narrator continues to trust in Bledsoe, illustrating that he has still not fully learned to look beneath surfaces. He overlooks Bledsoe's propensity for double-dealing precisely when he should most remember it.

Thus, we see that Bledsoe uses masks not only to dupe the white establishment but to dupe his own students. The narrator's grandfather advised his family to use masks as a form of self-defense and resistance against racist white power, but Bledsoe uses masks as a weapon against members of his own race. Moreover, he uses deception to achieve an influential position within the white-dominated power structure rather than to dismantle that structure. One can argue that Bledsoe's character shows the ultimate limitations of the grandfather's philosophy: African Americans will not win true power for themselves as a people if they continue to lead double lives.

Yet, while Ellison may imply that active duplicity and illusion may not lead to freedom and dignity, he suggests that African Americans should nonetheless remain aware of their power, if only to be on guard against them. This message comes across in the episode of Barbee's sermon. The sermon reinforces total allegiance to the college's and Bledsoe's (outward) philosophy. Barbee regards the Founder as a god of sorts, whose ideology should be trusted completely, like a religion. The sermon declares that the Founder's ideology and life represent a universal example that should be followed blindly rather than skillfully manipulated, as Bledsoe does. This blind faith and blind allegiance becomes physically embodied in the character of Barbee—a blind man. Ellison implicitly compares Barbee, whose first name is Homer, to the legendary blind Greek poet Homer, who composed the Odyssey and the Iliad. Barbee's sermon, an appreciative tribute to the Founder, attempts a project similar to that of Homer's two epic poems, which celebrate the Greek heroes Odysseus and Achilles, respectively.

The story of the Founder's physical impotence emphasizes the powerlessness that arises from a policy of blind faith. If the Founder himself—this figurehead of the college's power and glory—is sterile, then the fertility of his vision and legacy comes into question. His legacy's offspring include a blind preacher, the double-dealing Bledsoe, and a narcissistic Boston philanthropist who refuses to acknowledge what seems to be an incestuous attraction to his deceased daughter. The Founder's name is lost to history, and he becomes an empty symbol manipulated by men like Bledsoe to preserve the blindness of others. The reverent sermon revives the narrator's blind love and devotion to the college and to its program; however, this devotion prompts the narrator to trust blindly in the self-interested Bledsoe. While reprimanding the narrator for his carelessness with Norton, Bledsoe toys with an antique slave shackle, noting that it symbolizes African-American progress. By the end of these chapters, however, Bledsoe's shackle becomes a symbol of continuing enslavement to multiple forms of blindness.

CHAPTERS 7–9

SUMMARY: CHAPTER 7
On the bus to New York, the narrator encounters the veteran who mocked Mr. Norton and the college. Dr. Bledsoe has arranged to have the man transferred to a psychiatric facility in Washington, D.C. The narrator cannot believe that Bledsoe could have anything to do with the transfer, but the veteran winks and tells him to learn to see under the surface of things. He tells the narrator to hide himself from white people, from authority, from the invisible man who is pulling his strings. Crenshaw, the veteran's attendant, tells him that he talks too much. The veteran replies that he verbalizes things that most men only feel. Before switching to another bus, the veteran advises the narrator to serve as his own father. The narrator arrives in New York and gazes with astonishment at a black officer directing white drivers in the street. He sees a gathering on a sidewalk in Harlem, in which a man with a West Indian accent (whom he later learns is Ras the Exhorter) gives a speech about "chasing them [the whites] out." The narrator feels as though a riot might erupt at any minute. He quickly finds a place called the Men's House and takes a room.

SUMMARY: CHAPTER 7
Over the next few days, the narrator delivers all of the letters of recommendation that Bledsoe gave him except for one, which is addressed to a Mr. Emerson. A week passes, but he receives no response. He tries to telephone the addressees, all trustees of the college, only to receive polite refusals from their secretaries. His money is running out, and he begins to entertain vague doubts about Bledsoe's motives.

SUMMARY: CHAPTER 9
The narrator sets out to deliver his last letter and meets a man named Peter Wheatstraw, who speaks in a black dialectical banter and recognizes the narrator's Southern roots. Wheatstraw describes Harlem as a bear's den, which reminds the narrator of the folk stories of Jack the Rabbit and Jack the Bear. The narrator stops for breakfast at a deli. The waiter says he looks like he would enjoy the special: pork chops, grits, eggs, hot biscuits, and coffee. Insulted by the waiter's stereotyping, the narrator orders orange juice, toast, and coffee.

The narrator arrives at Mr. Emerson's office. He meets Emerson's son, a nervous little man. The son takes the letter and goes off to read it, only to return with a vaguely disturbed expression, chattering about his analyst and about injustice. Finally, the son allows the narrator to read the letter: Bledsoe has told each of the addressees that the narrator has earned permanent expulsion and that Bledsoe had to send him away under false pretenses in order to protect the college; Bledsoe requests that the narrator be allowed to "continue undisturbed in [his] vain hopes [of returning to college] while remaining as far as possible from our midst." Emerson says that his father is a strict, unforgiving man and that he will not help the narrator, but he offers to secure the narrator a job at the Liberty Paints plant. The narrator leaves the office full of anger and a desire for revenge. He imagines Bledsoe requesting that Emerson "hope the bearer of this letter to death and keep him running." He calls the plant and is told to report to work the next morning.

ANALYSIS: CHAPTERS 7–9

During the time in which the novel is set, Booker T. Washington's philosophy that blacks should put their energy toward achieving economic success rather than agitate for social equality reigned in the South as the predominant ideology for the advancement of black Americans. Both white and black Southerners embraced this approach at the time. At the Golden Day in Chapter 3, the veteran succinctly points out the blindness and enslavement that this philosophy entails, and Bledsoe expels him from the South just as he expels the narrator. Unlike the narrator, however, the veteran has desired such a relocation for years. He has used free speech to defy the masquerade and, accordingly, has won the freedom that he desired. The veteran's success, however, is merely a Pyrrhic victory—his trip north leads only to further confinement in another asylum.

In his attempt to clarify the American power system for the narrator, the veteran revisits the doll or marionette motif with the image of important men pulling strings. Those controlling the narrator's life remain invisible, hidden behind masks; pulling his strings, they treat him like an object rather than an individual human being. In his belief that these puppet masters are white, however, the veteran fails to recognize the manner in which black men like Bledsoe wield the same sort of control over other blacks. But while Bledsoe manipulates the self-understanding of his students, he himself seems blind to his own role as a tool of the white hierarchy. He believes that he achieves power for himself as a black man; rather than dismantle the white-dominated power structure, however, he only reinforces and reproduces it.

The narrator, on the other hand, seeks to escape this power structure. He begins an archetypal journey—the great migration north in search of freedom. New York immediately presents itself as a world vastly different from that of the South: the narrator marvels, for example, at Ras the Exhorter, whose inflammatory call for the black Harlem residents to drive out the whites would surely get him lynched in the South. Ras's ideology of black nationalism and of complete distrust of white people is wholly new to the naïve narrator.

Despite the greater scope of black freedom that he witnesses, the narrator cannot shed his experience of prejudice as quickly as he would like. He encounters reminders of his southern heritage in the figure of Peter Wheatstraw and in the deli, when the waiter rather prejudicially suggests that he would like a stereotypically Southern meal. These reminders in themselves, however, may not prove the most serious encroachment on the narrator's freedom; rather, his continued enslavement may stem from his disavowal of what these reminders represent. To disown his Southern origins is to disown a part of himself, to repress a part of his identity.

Bledsoe's betrayal of the narrator seems initially to put Ras's philosophy of complete distrust for whites into question, as it overlooks the fact that blacks can betray blacks. But Bledsoe's outlook subtly strengthens Ras's case, for he ultimately remains loyal to the white-dominated power structure, as his selfishness leads him to betray the narrator. One can view his treachery, then, as a triumph by the white hierarchy—in encouraging conformism among blacks, Bledsoe himself serves merely as a pawn. Emerson's son suggests to the narrator that he see this betrayal as an opportunity. By expelling the narrator and ensuring his banishment from the white trustees' circles of influence in New York, Bledsoe may have inadvertently done the narrator a favor: this banishment could mean a new freedom. Free of men like Emerson's father, the narrator may be able to redefine himself properly.

CHAPTER 10

SUMMARY

*"Our white is so white you can paint a chunka coal
and you'd have to crack it open with a sledge hammer
to prove it wasn't white clear through."*
(See QUOTATIONS, p. 70)

The narrator arrives at the Liberty Paints plant. A huge electric sign reads "KEEP AMERICA PURE WITH LIBERTY PAINTS." The narrator's supervisor, Mr. Kimbro, leads him to a long room filled with buckets of paint. Kimbro demonstrates the job: he opens buckets filled with a foul, milky brown substance and drips ten drops of another black chemical into them; then he stirs the buckets vigorously until the paint becomes glossy white; last, he applies the paint to small, rectangular wooden boards and waits for them to dry. If they dry brilliant white, then the job has been done correctly. Kimbro brags that the Optic White of Liberty Paints is the purest white that can be found anywhere. He says that it can cover up almost anything.

When only a little of the black chemical remains, Kimbro instructs the narrator to go to the tank room to get more. There, however, the narrator finds seven tanks marked by incomprehensible codes, leaving him unable to determine which tank contains the right chemical. He chooses one by scent and continues to mix and paint the tiles, but the tiles turn out sticky and gray, not hard and glossy. Kimbro returns and becomes infuriated, scolding the narrator for putting concentrated remover into the paint and thereby ruining some seventy-five buckets of paint. Kimbro fills the dropper with the correct chemical and leaves the narrator to his job. The paint samples still dry with a vague gray tinge, but Kimbro doesn't seem to notice.

Later, the narrator is sent to the furnace room to assist the engineer, Lucius Brockway. Brockway, who believes that assistants are always college-educated men who want to usurp his job, declares that he doesn't need an assistant but sets the narrator to work anyway. He instructs the narrator to watch the pressure gauges on the boiler. Brockway takes pride in his indispensable role in making Optic White paint, Liberty Paint's trademark color, since he alone can mix the base for the paint correctly. The slogan for the color is, "If It's Optic White, It's the Right White." The slogan reminds the narrator of an old Southern saying: "If you're white, you're right."

Lunchtime arrives, and the narrator returns to the locker room to retrieve his lunch, interrupting a union meeting. Some members accuse him of being a "fink," or an informer, when they hear that he is Brockway's assistant. The men resolve to investigate the narrator and then allow him to retrieve his lunch. When Brockway learns about the union meeting, he becomes furious and threatens to kill the narrator if he doesn't leave the plant. The narrator denies belonging to the union. Brockway and the narrator begin pummeling each other until Brockway loses his dentures while biting the narrator. Brockway blubbers about the union trying to steal his job. The narrator notices the boilers hissing, and Brockway shouts for him to turn the valve in order to lower the pressure. The narrator doesn't have the strength to do so, however, and the boiler explodes. The narrator falls unconscious under a pile of machinery and "stinking goo."

ANALYSIS

The narrator's experiences at the Liberty Paints plant give Ellison the chance to debunk a social and historical myth prevalent since before the Civil War—that of the North as the land of freedom for black Americans. The North, it turns out, perpetuates its own racist social structure, with which the narrator becomes further acquainted in the second half of the novel. The Liberty Paints plant serves as an extended metaphor for racial inequality in America. The factory's authorities, with their slogans emphasizing concepts of whiteness and purity, imply the moral superiority of their whiteness. The inclusion of "Liberty" in the factory's name emphasizes that the factory's leaders' notions reflect those held by the leaders of America, a country supposedly founded on "liberty" and equality but in fact, ironically, advocating more freedom for the individuals it deems worthiest.

When Brockway boasts that one would have to crack open a chunk of coal painted with Liberty Paints' Optic White in order to determine its black essence, he illustrates how blackness becomes invisible beneath whiteness at the plant. Mr. Kimbro brags that the paint's pure whiteness will cover anything, and indeed it covers the black chemical used to create it. That this specific shade of white is called "Optic" equates whiteness with clarity. This label is ironic, however, because the brilliance of the paint is blinding. Like a mask, the paint covers and conceals.

Ellison injects a great deal of similar irony into the portrayal of the Liberty Paints company. The necessity of mixing the base with the dead black chemical to produce the blinding white paint demonstrates that the brilliance of whiteness needs blackness. Moreover, the very success of the company's trademark Optic White paint results from the black Brockway's skill in mixing the base. The metaphor of Brockway's mixing implies that the dominance and privilege of whiteness derive from the abject status of blackness—whiteness couldn't occupy its privileged position signifying "purity," "liberty," and "rightness" without disempowering blackness.

Ellison also criticizes the racial inequality perpetuated by the social and political structures that operate within American companies and thus within American capitalism. While Brockway may have a certain position of influence in the company, his is not a position of power. He remains in constant fear of losing his job and scorns labor activists for their ingratitude. He advocates that the young, black college graduates who come to the plant be grateful to powerful white men for providing them with jobs and espouses an ideology resembling that of Booker T. Washington: be content with economic success and do not agitate for civil or political rights. Like Dr. Bledsoe, Brockway retains his position of influence by betraying the efforts of others to gain equality. He creates a shallow sense of empowerment by bragging about his indispensability to the company. His bravado is a mask for a deep sense of insecurity about his job and his position in society.

The narrator encounters the frustrating truth that coming to the North hasn't afforded him the freedom to define his own identity. The union members brand him a "fink," or informant, and vote to investigate him without allowing him to defend himself, and Brockway brands him a traitor and forces their confrontation to a violent resolution. Like the scene of the battle royal in Chapter 1, the portrayal of the conditions at Liberty Paints strongly contradicts Booker T. Washington's belief that economic advancement leads to freedom. Ellison insists that no amount of industriousness and hard work on the part of black Americans will grant them social or political equality, because whites will never grant them that equality out of sheer goodwill.

CHAPTER 11

SUMMARY

The narrator wakes in a hospital to see a man—a doctor—with what appears to be a bright third eye glowing in the center of his forehead. The narrator finds himself wearing a white pair of overalls. The doctor gives him something to swallow, and he loses consciousness again. Later, he wakes on a cot to see the third eye burning into his own eye. The doctor asks him for his name, but the narrator can only think about his pain. The "pink-faced" doctors begin using electrical shock treatment on him. The narrator cannot remember why he is in the hospital. He hears machines humming in the background and music that sounds like the cry of a woman in pain.

The doctors argue about how to proceed with the narrator: one wants to continue with the electrical shocks, while another believes that such means are rather primitive and argues that they wouldn't use electrical shocks on someone with a Harvard or New England background. The first doctor declares that electric shock will have the effect of a lobotomy (a surgical procedure that involves severing nerve fibers in the brain to alleviate certain mental disorders) and adds that both the narrator and society will be the better for this procedure. Someone suggests castration, but the doctor in charge chooses to continue with the electric shocks. As the shocks hit the narrator, someone muses that he is dancing, noting that "they [black people] really do have rhythm."

The doctors ask the narrator a question, but he cannot understand the words. They write their question down on a card: WHAT IS YOUR NAME? The narrator realizes that he cannot remember his name. The doctors barrage him with other written questions relating to his identity, but the narrator can respond with only a mute stare. Asked his mother's name, he can think only that a mother is "one who screams when you suffer," and again he hears the screams of the hospital machines.

The doctors then write: WHO WAS BUCKEYE THE RABBIT? The narrator thinks in confused, angry amusement that he is Buckeye the Rabbit, and he becomes annoyed to think that the doctor has hit upon his old identity. The doctors ask: BOY, WHO WAS BRER RABBIT? The narrator thinks sarcastically, "He was your mother's backdoor man." He adds that Brer and Buckeye are "one and the same: 'Buckeye' when you were very young and . . . innocent . . . 'Brer,' when you were older."

The narrator learns that he is in the factory hospital. The doctors tell him that he is cured and should dress and sign some papers in order to receive his compensation check. The director of the hospital urges him to find a quieter, easier job, since he is not ready for the difficulties of factory work. The narrator asks whether the director knows Mr. Norton or Dr. Bledsoe, joking that they are old friends of his.

The narrator leaves the hospital feeling as though an "alien personality" has taken hold of him. Roaming around in a trance-like stupor, he realizes that he has overcome his fear of important men like the trustees and Bledsoe. He wanders into the subway and sees a platinum blonde woman biting a red apple as the train heads for Harlem.

ANALYSIS

The narrator's experiences in the hospital mark an important transition in *Invisible Man,* as the narrator experiences a figurative rebirth. Ellison fills this chapter with imagery equating the narrator with a newborn child—he wakes with no memory, an inability to understand speech, and a wholly unformed identity. The background music and noise made by the machines combine to sound like a woman moaning in pain, evoking the cries of a woman in labor. This rebirth, however, involves no parents: the narrator faces the doctors alone. The conspicuous lack of mother or father recalls the veteran's advice that the narrator should be his own father—that is, create his own identity rather than accept an identity imposed on him from the outside. This rebirth scene signals the transformation of the narrator's character as he moves into a different phase of his life. Having lost his job at the plant—his last remaining connection to the college—he can now remake his identity.

The narrator's relationship with the hospital doctors dramatizes the consequences of invisibility and blindness as they are portrayed throughout the novel. Because the narrator has temporarily lost the ability to speak, his doctors are unable to learn anything about his identity, and because he has amnesia, he himself knows very little about who he is. As the scene progresses and the white doctors continue to fail to ascertain any information about their black patient, they increasingly fall back on racial stereotypes, collapsing him into a caricature, a kind of dancing Sambo doll like the ones that Tod Clifton sells in Chapter 20. As the narrator suffers the spasms of electric shock therapy, the doctors note caustically that black people have excellent rhythm. This stereotyping comment also revives the marionette metaphor: the doctors attach the narrator to various strings (wires) through which the electric current passes, and he "danc[es]" on cue when they send an electric current through his body. This electrical shock treatment recalls the electrified rug in the Chapter 1, on which the narrator writhes and contorts to the amusement of white onlookers spouting racist beliefs. Similarly, in that episode the narrator recalls seeing one of the other black boys "literally danc[ing] upon his back" and coming out of the spasm with an ashen face.

The references to Southern folk culture in this chapter hearken back to earlier references of the same type, though they now have a different effect on the narrator. In Chapter 9, when the narrator meets the jive-talking Peter Wheatstraw and recalls Brer Rabbit and Brer Bear (two characters from folktales introduced to America by African slaves), the encounter makes him smile "despite himself" as he feels a flash of mixed pride and disgust. Now, however, the doctors' inquiries about the folklore characters help the narrator to recover some of his memory. The narrator is reborn, but his heritage follows him into his new life. Yet, while he remains unable to shed his culture as he transforms his identity, he also proves unable to free himself from the burden of racism. For while Southern black folklore constitutes a rich part of who he is, it also differentiates him from white people, and the racist doctors use this difference as an excuse to violate the narrator and deny his humanity. Perhaps the most sinister manifestation of the doctors' racism lies in the suggestion of castrating the narrator. Symbolically, to castrate someone is to strip him of his power, to strip him of his ability to leave a genetic legacy; a systematic castration of all black males would be tantamount to genocide.

The idea of castration echoes the accidental sterilization of the Founder, another nameless black man who has been transformed into a stereotype. It also underscores white America's hidden obsession with black sexuality, which we see in Mr. Norton's bizarre curiosity about Jim Trueblood's incest. As evidenced in Chapter 1, the lurid interest of white men in black sexuality tends to revolve around the idea of black men lusting after white women, a stereotype that Ellison subtly references when he portrays the narrator watching the blonde woman nibble at the apple on the subway. The allusion to this stereotype foreshadows the narrator's eventual sexual encounters with white women. Moreover, the apple in this episode figures significantly. According to the Bible, God instructed Adam and Eve not to eat any fruit from the Tree of Knowledge, but Eve disobeys and then persuades Adam to partake of the forbidden fruit as well. Similarly, in this episode, society strictly forbids any sexual desire that the narrator might feel for the blonde woman.

At the end of this chapter, the narrator's invisibility has made him freer, even if it has not fully liberated him. As he sets out in New York, the narrator employs the veteran's advice to hide himself by being in the open, to achieve a greater measure of freedom, to define his own identity, to become his own father, so to speak. The narrator's ability to speak irreverently of men like Bledsoe and Norton demonstrates that he has overcome his blind devotion to the college and the ideology that rules it. Like the veteran, he no longer feels compelled to treat this slavish ideology with respect. Consequently, as he leaves the hospital, the narrator feels stronger, no longer afraid.

Chapters 12–15

Summary: Chapter 12

The narrator leaves the subway and collapses on the street. Several people help to carry him to the home of a kind black woman named Mary. When he wakes, she asks him why he came to New York City from the South. He replies that he wanted to be an educator. She cautions against the city's corrupting influence—she, too, came from the South—and says, "I'm in New York, but New York ain't in me." The narrator gets up to leave, and Mary tells him that he should come back if he ever wants to rent a room somewhere besides the Men's House, adding that she offers a fair rent.

The narrator's white overalls draw hostile stares at the Men's House. He knows that he can no longer live there. He scorns the ideals of older advocates of racial progress still mired in their dreams of black business empires; he pities those who still believe in the post–Civil War dreams of freedom within segregation. He mocks those who work insignificant jobs but don expensive clothing and affect the manners of courtly Southern congressmen, hoping to cover up their low social status.

As he heads for the elevator, the narrator sees a laughing man whom he mistakes for Dr. Bledsoe. He promptly empties a spittoon on the man's head but then discovers that his victim is a prominent Baptist preacher. He escapes before anyone can catch him. He later persuades an amused porter to retrieve his belongings from inside the building and learns that the Men's House has banned him for ninety-nine years and a day. The narrator takes a room at Mary's apartment. He bristles with irritation at her constant expectation that he will take up some leadership role in the black community. Yet she never criticizes him when he fails to do so, or when he cannot pay for food or rent. The narrator begins to feel the desire for activism anyhow; within himself he feels a "spot of black anger." His old urge to give speeches returns as winter settles over New York.

SUMMARY: CHAPTER 13

The narrator encounters a street vendor selling baked yams and experiences a sudden nostalgia for the South. He buys three to eat as he walks down the street, feeling totally free. He imagines his classmates' shock at seeing him with these emblems of Southern culture. He scorns them for distancing themselves from all of the things that they in fact like: yams, chitterlings, and boiled hog's maws. He comes upon a crowd of people gathered to watch as an eviction takes place. The crowd regards this act of dispossession as a common occurrence. White men drag household furnishings out of an apartment and lug one chair out the door with an old black woman still sitting in it. Looking at the contents of the old woman's and her husband's lives scattered roughly across the pavement, the narrator identifies acutely with the couple. He becomes angry and spontaneously delivers a rousing speech that incites the crowd to resistance. The crowd then carries the couple's belongings back into the building.

The police arrive, and the narrator flees. He thinks that he has successfully escaped when he hears a voice behind him: "That was a masterful bit of persuasion, brother." The voice belongs to a white man, who claims he is a friend. He takes the narrator to a coffeehouse and tries to persuade him to become a paid spokesperson for his political organization's Harlem branch. The narrator turns him down; the man tells him that his name is Brother Jack and gives him a phone number to call should he change his mind.

SUMMARY: CHAPTER 14

The narrator changes his mind as soon as he returns to Mary's home, realizing that she has been housing and feeding him for free since his compensation check from the factory ran out weeks earlier. He calls the number that Jack gave him and agrees to meet him on Lenox Avenue. A car pulls up with Jack and several other men inside. They drive to a hotel called the Chthonian, where a cocktail party seems to be taking place. Jack introduces the narrator to his mistress, Emma, who whispers not quite softly enough to Jack, "But don't you think he should be a little blacker?"

Jack explains that his organization, called the Brotherhood, focuses on social activism, banding together to fight for people who have been "dispossessed of their heritage." He says that the narrator will be given some documents to read to help him decide whether to join the Brotherhood. He asks the narrator if he would like to be the new Booker T. Washington and rambles on about an impending world crisis, declaring that destruction lies ahead if social changes are not made—changes that have to be brought about by the people.

The narrator accepts the position, and Jack informs him that he must change his name, move to an apartment provided by the Brotherhood, and make a complete break with his past. Jack writes down the narrator's new name on a slip of paper and gives it to him. "This is your new identity," he says. He also gives the narrator three hundred dollars for back rent, and explains that he will receive sixty dollars a week, a large sum. The narrator returns to Mary's apartment late that night.

SUMMARY: CHAPTER 15

> [T]he cast-iron figure of a very black, red-lipped and
> wide-mouthed Negro . . . his face an enormous grin . . .
> (See QUOTATIONS, p. 71)

The next morning, the narrator notices for the first time an object standing next to his door: a cast-iron coin bank in the form of a black man with bright red lips. If one places a coin into the statue's hand and presses a lever on the back, the coin flips into the grinning mouth. The narrator breaks the statue in a fury but then cleans up the pieces, along with the coins that scatter on the floor. Ashamed to tell Mary about his deed, he gathers the debris in an old newspaper and hides the package in his coat pocket. He pays his debt and leaves Mary's house without telling her that he will not return.

The narrator throws the package into a garbage can outside, but an old woman demands that he take his trash out of her can. He leaves the package in the snow at an intersection. Another man, thinking that the narrator has left the package behind accidentally, follows him across the street and gives it back to him. The narrator finally drops the package into his briefcase and gets onto the subway. He notices people reading newspapers that declare in bold headlines: "Violent Protest Over Harlem Eviction." He buys a new suit and calls Jack, who instructs him to go to his new apartment on the Upper East Side, where he will find literature on the Brotherhood awaiting his perusal. Jack wants the narrator to give a speech at a Harlem rally scheduled for that evening.

ANALYSIS: CHAPTERS 12–15

By the time the narrator returns to the Men's House, he has made a break with Booker T. Washington's philosophy that economic opportunities lead to freedom. This break is evidenced by his aggression toward the man who he momentarily believes to be Dr. Bledsoe. The narrator's white overalls from the hospital recall the rebirth that he experienced there and his subsequent change in outlook. He mocks other blacks for their careful attempts to cover up their low social standing; he believes that those who spend their meager wages on expensive clothing just to look wealthy and sophisticated are merely enslaving themselves to shallow consumerism.

After the narrator's figurative rebirth in Chapter 11, his relationship with Mary represents his second childhood, a rebuilding of his identity. In a sense, Mary is a mother figure. She prepares the narrator for his entry into society and helps him reclaim his Southern heritage. Her name, too, seems symbolic, evoking Mother Mary and images of the Virgin Mary cradling the baby Jesus. After living with Mary for a few months, the narrator embraces his heritage and revels in eating baked yams, a food symbolic of Southern black culture. Whereas he devoted himself at college to the prescribed role of the model black citizen, affecting the sophistication of white culture rather than the perceived barbarism of black culture, the narrator now rejects that affectation and chooses to behave as he wishes, seizing his freedom and celebrating his own background. He returns to the culture of his childhood, which the college tried to strip from him.

The narrator's embracing of his heritage occurs almost in tandem with his outrage at the eviction of the old black couple. When he sees mementos from the couple's life strewn out over the pavement, he recognizes that he and they share a culture. He realizes that in conforming to the college's ideology he had been accepting a value system contrary to this culture. His speech at the eviction doesn't rely on empty abstractions and mythical symbolism as does Reverend Barbee's earlier sermon about the Founder; nor is it riddled with vagueness, as is Jack's description of the Brotherhood's goals, which include fighting an "impending world crisis" and making unspecified "changes." Rather, the narrator's speech affirms his individuality in the context of the collective black American experience, one that he has recently come to embrace.

Yet, in joining the Brotherhood the narrator stands poised to abandon his heritage once again. By granting the narrator membership in a social and political movement, the Brotherhood temptingly revives his dreams of living a life of social significance. Additionally, the narrator's position within the organization provides him with the opportunity to do what he loves most—impassioned public speaking. However, it soon becomes clear that the Brotherhood is using the narrator as a means toward its own ends. Emma's comment to Jack that the narrator should be "blacker" indicates that the members of the Brotherhood relate to the narrator not as an individual human being but rather as an abstract symbol of his race. The Brotherhood calls on the narrator to assume a new identity and to break with his past, and he does so without resistance. That the hotel where the meeting takes place is named the Chthonian, a term that refers to the gods of the Greek underworld, symbolizes the sinister nature of the Brotherhood's intentions.

The episode with the coin bank, coming immediately after the narrator's decision to join the Brotherhood, seems to foreshadow a troubling relationship between the narrator and the Brotherhood. Although the narrator smashes the figurine in a rage against its offensive portrayal of blacks, his inability to rid himself of its fragments reflects his inability to escape the racism that the bank—and, as soon becomes clear, the Brotherhood—embodies. Indeed, the symbolism of this episode may serve not only to depict the persistent influence of racism but also to pass judgment on the narrator for submitting himself to it. For while the narrator seems doomed to live with the vestiges of Southern racism, the text suggests that the narrator is also willingly but unwittingly acting out the stereotype that the bank perpetuates—that of the grinning, obedient slave. In joining the Brotherhood and complaisantly agreeing to serve as their black advocate, the narrator allows himself to be seen as an abstraction of "blackness." He subverts his own individuality in order to meet the expectations of powerful white men. That the narrator finally puts the fragments of the bank into the same briefcase that

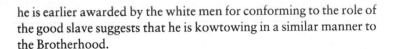

he is earlier awarded by the white men for conforming to the role of the good slave suggests that he is kowtowing in a similar manner to the Brotherhood.

CHAPTERS 16–17

SUMMARY: CHAPTER 16

Members of the Brotherhood drive the narrator to a rally, telling him to hold off his speech until the crowd becomes frenzied. The rally takes place in a former boxing ring. The narrator notices a torn photograph of a former prizefight champion who lost his vision during a rigged fight and later died in a home for the blind. As the narrator climbs the ramp to the stage, the spotlight blinds him temporarily. The crowd chants, "No more dispossessing of the dispossessed!" As the narrator steps to the microphone, the glaring light prevents him from seeing the audience. In his nervousness, he forgets all of the catchphrases that he has read in the literature of the Brotherhood and decides to improvise.

The narrator's speech plays on an extended metaphor of blindness and aligns itself along a dichotomy of "they" and "we." In his oratory, the narrator says that "they" have dispossessed each one of "us" of an eye. "We" walk down the sidewalks, he says, blind on one side, while an oily scoundrel in the middle of the street throws stones at "us." The narrator calls to the crowd to regain "our" sight and band together so that "we" might see both sides of the street. The audience applauds thunderously when he finishes. He steps blindly from the platform, stumbling into the arms of his admirers.

Afterward, some of the Brothers criticize his speech for its inflammatory, unscientific style. They decide to send the narrator to Brother Hambro to nurture his natural talent for speaking but infuse it with the rhetoric of the Brotherhood. The narrator returns home feeling like a new person, radically different from the boy expelled from college. Yet, in his moment of pride and triumph, memories of his grandfather fleetingly haunt him.

SUMMARY: CHAPTER 17

After the narrator has studied the Brotherhood's ideology intensely for months, the committee votes to appoint him as chief spokesperson for the Harlem district. The narrator receives his own office and meets Tod Clifton, a black member of the executive committee, who informs him that Ras the Exhorter, a militant black nationalist, remains the chief opponent of the Brotherhood in Harlem.

Ras—whom the narrator sees giving an impassioned speech when he first arrives in New York—calls for complete and utter distrust of white culture.

One day, the Brotherhood holds a rally in protest of what it deems to be racist eviction policies in Harlem. Ras and his followers disrupt the rally, and a brawl ensues. In the darkness of the night, the narrator has difficulty distinguishing his followers from those of Ras. He finds Clifton and Ras locked in an intense fight. Ras pulls a knife but decides to spare Clifton, citing their common skin color. He asks Clifton why he works with the Brotherhood, in which black members constitute the minority, and accuses him of turning his back on his heritage. He insinuates that the Brotherhood lured Clifton with the promise of white women and warns that the white members of the Brotherhood will eventually betray the black members.

The narrator begins calling Harlem community leaders for support in the Brotherhood's fight against unfair eviction. These leaders all fall in line behind the Brotherhood on the issue. The narrator's new name becomes well known in the community. He throws himself into his work, organizing marches and rallies. Yet he still has nightmares about Dr. Bledsoe, Lucius Brockway, and his grandfather, and he feels a profound split between his public and private selves.

ANALYSIS: CHAPTERS 16–17

In his speech at the rally in Chapter 16, the narrator uses an extended metaphor of blindness to illustrate oppression. Blindness has divided oppressed people throughout the novel: the college's faculty and students disowned Jim Trueblood because of their blind allegiance to an ideology; Bledsoe betrays the narrator for the same reason. Brockway betrays the union due to his fear of losing his job and his naive faith in the ability of white power structures to help him maintain his position. At the same time, the union refuses to allow the narrator to speak for himself, and does so out of its own utter distrust of the black Brockway. The narrator calls for an end to the blindness that causes such interracial divisions and urges the formation of a united front. His speech, however, becomes ironic when we learn that he cannot even see his audience; he becomes a blind leader of a blind audience. The narrator stumbles blindly as he leaves the microphone, just as Reverend Barbee does after his sermon in Chapter 5, and as the prizefighter must have done after his blinding bout in the ring.

Some members of the Brotherhood become dissatisfied with the speech's lack of "scientific" content—their term for abstract rhetoric and ideological jargon. The narrator has spoken freely as an individual rather than as the propaganda tool that they would have him be. The narrator agrees to have Brother Hambro "educate" him, but he fails to see the similarities between this education and the one that he received in college: though he believes in each as a means toward advancement—in college, his own advancement; in Harlem, the advancement of his people—each requires his blind adherence to an ideology imposed from the outside, and each squelches his individual identity.

The first rally that the narrator attends as the Brotherhood's Harlem spokesperson contains additional ominous signs that his involvement with the Brotherhood will not be promising. The narrator's inability to differentiate between his followers and Ras's, in the nighttime brawl that breaks out in Chapter 17, seems a sign of the unproductiveness of this confrontation, since both groups are fighting for black advancement. Ellison does not condone Ras's violence; however, Ras's gesture of sparing Clifton because of their shared skin color is a concrete demonstration of respect for a black man, whereas the speeches that the narrator makes for the Brotherhood are abstract and help blacks in a much less immediate way. The nightmares that the narrator experiences about his old life seem to evidence a subconscious feeling that the Brotherhood, as Ras predicts, will eventually betray him.

Although the narrator initially believes that his membership in the Brotherhood has made him into a new person, his nightmares about figures from the past suggest that his past cannot be erased and that it will continue to haunt him. By dedicating himself to his work, the narrator has indeed gained a well-known public identity. However, he suffers intense internal conflict between his public and private selves, and consequently feels as if he is "running a foot race" against himself. The narrator's observation echoes his dream in Chapter 1 in which he opens his briefcase to find the envelope containing a paper that reads "Keep This Nigger-Boy Running." Clearly, the Brotherhood's attempt to refashion the narrator's identity doesn't celebrate his individuality but rather keeps him running, searching to define himself against stereotypes.

While Ras correctly intuits an underlying racism among the Brotherhood's leadership, his own black nationalist philosophy offers a similarly specious liberation. Like the ideologies of the Brotherhood and the narrator's college, it demands that individuals break completely with their past and submit to someone else's definition of their identity.

CHAPTERS 18–19

SUMMARY: CHAPTER 18

The narrator receives an anonymous, unstamped letter telling him not to "go too fast" and to remember that he is still a black man in a white world. He asks another black member of the Brotherhood, Brother Tarp, if anyone in the organization dislikes him. Tarp assures him that he is well liked and says that he doesn't know who wrote the letter. Tarp asks the narrator if he comes from the South. Tarp then confides in him that he spent nineteen years in a black chain gang for having said "no" to a white man. He gives the narrator a leg iron to remind him of their real cause.

Another black member of the group, Brother Wrestrum, glimpses the leg iron on the narrator's desk and suggests that he put it away because it "dramatizes" the racial differences in the Brotherhood. Wrestrum hints that some members of the Brotherhood hold racist attitudes, but the narrator disregards him. Wrestrum then suggests that every member of the Brotherhood wear a symbol so that the Brothers can recognize their own members: Tod Clifton once beat up a white Brother during a street brawl after mistaking him for one of the hoodlums trying to quash a Brotherhood rally.

A magazine editor calls the office to request an interview with the narrator. The narrator tries to persuade the editor to interview Clifton instead, but the editor cites the narrator's favorable public image; he wants to give his readers a hero figure. The narrator explains that every Brother is a cog in the machine, each sacrificing personal ambitions for the benefit of the whole organization. Wrestrum silently encourages the narrator as he expresses these sentiments. However, the narrator yields and agrees to the interview, partly to spite the overbearing Wrestrum. Wrestrum leaves the office.

Two weeks later, Wrestrum accuses the narrator of using the Brotherhood to further his own personal ambitions. He points to the magazine interview as evidence. The narrator considers Wrestrum's face a mask: behind the mask, he imagines, the real Wrestrum is laughing. The committee finds the narrator innocent in regard to the magazine article but decides to conduct a thorough investigation of his other work with the Brotherhood. They transfer him downtown, out of the Harlem District, and make him a women's rights spokesperson for the duration of the investigation. Although disappointed, the narrator decides to dedicate himself fully to his new assignment. He packs his papers into his briefcase and leaves.

SUMMARY: CHAPTER 19

After the narrator's first lecture as a women's rights activist, a white woman invites him into her home to discuss the Brotherhood's ideology. She turns out to be a neglected wife who aims to seduce him. She and the narrator sleep together. Later in the night, the woman's husband comes home. Since the husband and wife sleep in separate bedrooms, he simply pokes his head inside her darkened room, briefly asking her to wake him early in the morning. When the wife bids him a good night's rest, he returns the sentiment, but with a short dry laugh. The narrator dresses and rushes from the building, unsure of whether he dreamed the husband, and incredulous that the husband seemed not to notice him. He vows never to get himself into such a situation again.

The Brotherhood summons the narrator to an emergency meeting. The members inform him that he will be transferred back to Harlem and that Clifton has disappeared. The Brotherhood has lost popularity in Harlem, while Ras has gained an ever larger following. Jack tells the narrator that he must attend a strategy meeting the next day.

ANALYSIS: CHAPTERS 18–19

Much of Ellison's novel contemplates the advantages and disadvantages of invisibility; in Chapter 18, the narrator learns a lesson about visibility. He recognizes the extent of his visibility when he receives the anonymous letter. The letter's author echoes a sentiment similar to that of the Southern whites, Bledsoe, and others—don't fight too hard too fast for racial equality. By making himself a prominent figure in his contribution to the Brotherhood's fight for social equality, the narrator may have gained power for his movement, but he also puts himself in jeopardy. In contrast, the letter writer gains power over the narrator by remaining invisible. Later in the chapter, the narrator again learns the dangers of visibility when Wrestrum accuses him of opportunism regarding the magazine interview—he objects to the narrator's high profile and public image.

Brother Tarp's dark past belies the notion that one can escape the South's racist legacy by fleeing to the North. Although he escaped the brutal conditions of the chain gang, Tarp continues to suffer from the wounds that he incurred during his nineteen years of slavery; his persistent limp attests to these wounds' permanence. Though no longer enslaved, he still walks as if in chains. He also believes in the importance of remembering this dark past: although he limps involuntarily, he quite deliberately chooses to keep his shackle as a reminder of his bondage. Like the narrator's grandfather, he cautions the narrator never to become too complacent about his freedom; he gives the narrator his shackle to help him follow this advice. Tarp's shackle recalls the shackle that Dr. Bledsoe keeps on his desk at the college. Yet Tarp's shackle lies twisted and rusted from authentic use; Bledsoe's attests to no personal past but, rather, serves as a superficial, inauthentic decoration. Bledsoe's unbroken shackle symbolizes the continuing legacy of slavery, while Tarp's shackle, broken open during his escape, signifies the freedom of a fugitive prisoner.

When Brother Wrestrum advises the narrator to put the leg shackle out of sight, noting that it dramatizes the racial differences within the Brotherhood, he exhibits a blindness and ideology similar to that of Bledsoe and the narrator's college as an institution. The black college students emulate white culture and white values in return for the opportunity for social advancement. Much as the college students shun their black Southern cultural heritage and history, Wrestrum advises the narrator to hide this symbol of the brutal historical experiences of black Americans. Unlike Tarp, he wishes to forget and abandon that history. He believes servile invisibility will ease the racist attitudes of some of the Brotherhood's members. When he cites the incident in which Clifton mistakenly beat a white Brother during a brawl, he seems to do so with an eye to the white community's potential retaliation. In noting this possibility, he acknowledges the racist tendencies that permeate the North as well as the South. But Wrestrum would prefer to ignore rather than to address these racial tensions.

In the episode in which the narrator sleeps with the white woman, we see another instance of the North's veiled version of racism. In the South in which the novel is set, mixed meetings with both black and white social activists would probably not occur, and very few white women would consider sleeping with a black man. Yet, while this Northern white woman listens politely to the narrator's words, expresses admiration for him, and sleeps with him, she does not do so out of color blindness. Rather, to the white woman, the narrator embodies the "primitive" black male; she treats him as an object, using him to indulge her sexual fantasies.

CHAPTERS 20–21

SUMMARY: CHAPTER 20

The narrator visits a bar, one of his old Harlem haunts. He recognizes two men who have attended some of his speeches and addresses them as "brother." They react with hostility. He learns that many of the jobs that the Brotherhood procured for Harlem residents have disappeared. These men themselves have left the organization. Some men accuse the narrator of getting "white fever" when he moved to lecture downtown. He returns to his old office to look for Brother Tarp but fails to find anyone in the building. He discovers that Harlem membership in the Brotherhood has declined due to a change in the Brotherhood's emphasis from local issues to national and international concerns.

The narrator waits to be called to the strategy meeting that Brother Jack mentioned, but the call never comes. He hurries to headquarters anyway and finds the meeting already in progress. The narrator realizes that the other members intended to exclude him all along. Furious, he leaves the building and goes to shop for shoes. He spots Tod Clifton peddling "Sambo" dolls in the street. (The American stereotype of "Sambo" dates back to the time of slavery, denoting a docile but irresponsible, loyal but lazy slave.) Clifton sings out a jingle while the dolls dance in a loose-limbed motion. The narrator feels betrayed. Clifton sees some white police officers coming toward him and sweeps up his Sambo dolls, hastening around the corner. Apparently Clifton knows that he is not allowed to sell his dolls on the street. Clifton bids the audience that had gathered to watch his display to follow him. The narrator spots one of the dolls left behind and begins to crush it with his foot. Seeing one of the policemen nearby, however, he picks up the doll and puts it in his briefcase. He begins walking away, but as he comes around another corner he sees a huge crowd gathered. Clifton stands in the midst of it, flanked by policemen. The narrator then sees Clifton strike one of the officers, and the officer draws his gun and shoots Clifton dead.

SUMMARY: CHAPTER 21

The narrator returns to Harlem in a stunned daze, haunted by the memory of Clifton's death and of the black doll. Once he reaches his office, he tries to make the doll dance. He finally realizes that Clifton was manipulating it with a black string attached to its back. He stares at the doll until someone knocks at his door. A group of weeping young Brotherhood members asks him if Clifton is dead. The narrator confirms the story. He then tries to call the headquarters for instructions but receives no answer. He rallies the members in his building to stage a funeral march for Clifton and sends some women to claim the body from the morgue. He notifies the community churches of the funeral and publicizes Clifton's untimely, unnecessary death. When the march takes place two days later, the community is stirred and angry. Hundreds of former members of the Brotherhood show up to march. The narrator delivers a sobering speech to the audience. Once the speech is over, the narrator senses a heavy tension in the crowd. He hopes that members of the Brotherhood will harness that tension and recover their influence in the Harlem community.

ANALYSIS: CHAPTERS 20–21

These chapters focus sharply on the ideas of belonging and betrayal. While the narrator believes that he serves the interest of black Americans by joining with the Brotherhood, the former members of the Harlem branch shun him when he attempts to strike up a friendly conversation. They see his continued membership in the Brotherhood as a betrayal of the black community. On the other hand, the narrator himself feels betrayed in these chapters, first when he discovers Clifton selling the Sambo dolls and later when he learns that the Brotherhood has deliberately excluded him from their strategy meeting.

The men that the narrator encounters in the bar have left the Brotherhood in anger at the organization's gradual abandonment of the Harlem community. They thus distance themselves from the group's treachery, but, in the process, they lose their political voice. Clifton, too, has left the Brotherhood, again perhaps on principle; unlike these men, however, he does not fall silent but rather commits a worse treachery against his community. Not only do his puppets perpetuate stereotypes of blacks, but he also conforms to the represented stereotype by trying to please his audience in a servile way.

Nevertheless, Clifton's peddling of the dolls exhibits a more complex attitude toward race relations than a simple acceptance of stereotypes: he seems to offer a veiled commentary on the racial stereotype of the grinning, "yes"-saying "good slave" as he urges his listeners to stretch the doll by the neck and not worry about breaking it. Clifton intends to mock those who fulfill the stereotypical slave-master relationship with his assertion that the "good slave" lives for the sunshine of the white spectator's smile. On the other hand, he seems to sneer at those who think that they can escape the effects of this degrading stereotype. Clifton himself suffers the penalty for not confining himself to the "good slave" role. Though he defies white authority by rising up against the police officer, his deviation from his "proper" place leads immediately to his death. In the end, Clifton's selling of the dolls, whether undertaken as a last resort to fit into society or as a veiled act of defiance, proves much more dangerous than the other former Brotherhood members' retreat into silence.

The narrator's encounter with Clifton contains powerful symbolism. Although Clifton's Sambo dolls appear to move of their own accord, they actually move only when pulled from above by their strings. The text thus implies that black Americans continue to live like marionettes, their motions determined by white puppeteers. The stereotypes and expectations of a racist society compel them to behave only in certain ways, move according to certain patterns, never allowing them to act according to their own will. As Clifton pulls one of the doll's strings, he subtly ridicules the Brotherhood's ideology—"He'll kill your depression and your dispossession." The jingle-like quality of this assertion, which derives from the rhyme of "depression" and "dispossession," mocks the Brotherhood's aims and focuses the puppet metaphor on the Brotherhood. The narrator now realizes that the organization has used him as a tool.

Although the narrator now begins to understand that he cannot fight the white power structure by working within it, he remains unsure of how to assert himself effectively. He must find a way to operate outside of the white establishment without drifting into silence, settling into a stereotype, or provoking his own murder. The racism rampant in the current social structure keeps black Americans constantly on the outside while preempting any consolidation among the exiles, turning blacks against blacks. In such a society, the narrator is kept constantly running.

As the committee has excluded the narrator from its decision-making process, the narrator consciously chooses to act individually in regard to Clifton's funeral. During his eulogy, the narrator attributes Clifton's death specifically to racism; he doesn't speak in vague terms of general oppression, as is the tendency of Brother Jack. Moreover, the narrator repeatedly utters Clifton's name, emphasizing Clifton's own individual identity, which the Brotherhood attempted to strip from him. In doing so, the narrator hopes to engrave the memory of Clifton into the minds of the black community and thus impede his descent into invisibility.

CHAPTERS 22–23

SUMMARY: CHAPTER 22

The narrator returns to his office to find Brother Jack and the other committee members waiting for him. They are angry that he has associated the Brotherhood with the protest of Tod Clifton's death without the committee's approval. Jack informs the narrator that he was hired not to think but to talk—and to say only what the Brotherhood tells him to say. The Brotherhood officially regards Clifton as a traitor to the organization's ideals—Jack cites the group's alleged objection to Clifton's "anti-Negro" dolls—and would never have endorsed the eulogy that the narrator gave.

The narrator replies that the black community has accused the Brotherhood itself of betrayal. Jack says that the Brotherhood tells the community what to think. The narrator accuses Jack of trying to be the "great white father." Just then, one of Jack's eyes—a false one—pops out of his head into a drinking glass on the narrator's desk. He informs the narrator that he lost the eye while doing his duty, stating that his personal sacrifice proves his loyalty to the Brotherhood and its ideals. The argument winds down, and the committee takes its leave of the narrator. Jack instructs him to see Brother Hambro (a white member of the organization) to learn the Brotherhood's new program.

SUMMARY: CHAPTER 23

The Harlem community's outrage over Clifton's death continues to build. The narrator passes Ras (once known as "Ras the Exhorter," he now calls himself "Ras the Destroyer") giving a speech. Ras denounces the Brotherhood for not following through with the momentum that the funeral sparked. Two of Ras's followers briefly scuffle with the narrator, but the narrator escapes. In an attempt to disguise himself and protect himself from further physical attack, the narrator purchases a pair of sunglasses with dark green lenses. After he puts them on, a woman walks up to him and addresses him as "Rinehart." The narrator replies that he is not Rinehart, and she tells him to get away from her before he gets her into trouble.

The narrator augments his disguise with a large hat. As he makes his way back to Ras's meeting, several people address him as "Rinehart" again. A woman on the street thinks that he is Rinehart, her bookie; a prostitute thinks that he is Rinehart, her pimp; he passes a gathering of people waiting for "Reverend Rinehart," the "spiritual technologist," to hold a revival. The narrator is astounded at his ignorance of Rinehart's identity, with which apparently everyone else in the community is familiar.

The narrator finally reaches Brother Hambro's apartment. Hambro informs him that the Brotherhood intends to sacrifice its influence in the Harlem community to pursue other, wider political goals. The narrator leaves Hambro's apartment in a fury and decides to follow his grandfather's advice: he will "yes, agree, and grin the Brotherhood to death." He plans to assure the Brotherhood's members that the community stands in full agreement with their new policy and to fill out false membership cards to inflate the Brotherhood's Harlem membership. He also plans to discover the committee's real goals by cultivating a relationship with a woman close to one of the Brotherhood's important leaders. He thinks that perhaps he should try Emma, Jack's mistress.

ANALYSIS: CHAPTERS 22–23

At this point in the novel, the narrator finally loses the illusion that he can remain a free individual within the Brotherhood. He learns that the condition for membership in the Brotherhood is blind obedience to its ideology. Just as his college hired him to show Mr. Norton only what the college wanted Mr. Norton to see, the Brotherhood has hired him to say only what it wants people to hear, to be like the dancing Sambo doll, playing a role defined by the Brotherhood.

The Brotherhood's anger over the narrator's eulogy for Clifton reveals the committee members' own crippling blindness. If we interpret the white members' motivation for distancing themselves from Clifton as his connection to the racist dolls, then it becomes clear that they attach more political importance to a few offensive dolls than to the murder of Clifton. Ultimately, then, their way of rejecting racism only reproduces it: they end up condoning a racially motivated murder in an overzealous attempt to protect the Brotherhood's image as an antiracist organization. Their alleged idealism trivializes the concrete reality of racism, as they value the condemnation of abstract racist stereotypes over the condemnation of a racist murder. If, on the other hand, we interpret the offensiveness of Clifton's dolls as a mere pretense that Jack and the others use in order to break more cleanly from Harlem's interests, then it becomes clear that they are wholly blind to the undeniable need for the advancement of black political concerns.

The committee's blindness receives symbolic representation in the form of Jack's glass eye. Significantly, the eye falls out precisely as Jack describes the Brotherhood's ideological position. Thus, it symbolizes both the blindness of the group's ideology and the group's attempt to hide this blindness. Also significant is Jack's declaration that the loss of his eye proves his loyalty to the Brotherhood. The statement reveals Jack's conviction that blindness constitutes both the prerequisite and the price for full membership in the organization, for total adherence to its anti-individualist ideology. Moreover, this scene demonstrates that this blindness applies not only to the group's followers—such as the narrator—but also to its leaders.

Rinehart proves one of the strangest and most ambiguous figures in *Invisible Man;* though he never appears in the flesh, he serves as a powerful symbol of the idea of a protean or shape-shifting sense of identity, against which the narrator's own fragile sense of identity can be compared. Rinehart is all things to all people, and those individuals whom the narrator encounters while he wears his sunglasses impose a variety of identities upon him. This fluidity of character plays a major role in the narrator's crucial realization that he is invisible—that he has never had a self because he has always adopted a self given to him by others. Glimpsing Rinehart's endlessly malleable self, the narrator realizes for the first time that he does have his own self. He vows that, though he may remain invisible to others, he will from that moment forward be visible to himself. This breakthrough prepares him to endure not only his disillusioning confrontation with Hambro but also the hellish night of the Harlem riots and his confrontation with Ras the Destroyer in Chapter 25.

The narrator's conversation with Hambro shatters his remaining illusions about the Brotherhood. Hambro's description of the Brotherhood's plans, which prioritize the Brotherhood's larger goals over the will of the people, is veiled in the same vague, abstract language as all of the Brotherhood's ideology. Rather than view the Harlem community as a collection of individuals, the Brotherhood treats Harlem as a collective mass, an object to be manipulated for its own ends. Angry that he and his people have been exploited as instruments to others' ends, the narrator plots, ironically, to manipulate someone associated with the Brotherhood—namely Emma—for his own ends.

Chapters 24–Epilogue

Summary: Chapter 24

Crowds begin to form in Harlem at the slightest provocation; store windows are smashed and clashes erupt. Ras agitates the pointless violence further. The narrator sends out Brotherhood members to discourage the violence and denounces the press for exaggerating minor incidents. He reports at the Brotherhood headquarters that the Harlem branch has instituted a clean-up campaign to clear the neighborhood of trash and distract the people from Tod Clifton's death; he lies to them that Harlem has begun to quiet down and hands them a false list of new members. The Brotherhood fails to detect the narrator's deception.

The narrator decides against using Emma to discover the real goals of the Brotherhood. Instead, he decides to use Sybil, a neglected wife of one of the Brotherhood members, who had once indicated that she wanted to get to know him better. Inviting her to his apartment, he plans to act smooth and charming like Rinehart. He succeeds, however, only in getting himself and Sybil drunk. She has no interest in politics and only wants him to play a black savage in her rape fantasy.

The narrator suddenly receives a frantic call from the Brotherhood in Harlem, asking him to come as soon as possible. He hears the sound of breaking glass, and the line goes dead. He grabs his briefcase and puts Sybil in a cab headed downtown. He himself walks uptown toward Harlem. As he passes under a bridge, a flock of birds flies over him and covers him with droppings.

A riot erupts in Harlem. The narrator encounters a group of looters who give conflicting stories about what caused the initial outbreak. One mentions a young man "everyone is mad about," obviously referring to Clifton. Others mention Ras, while still others talk of a white woman having started the first clash.

SUMMARY: CHAPTER 25

> *I . . . recognized the absurdity of the whole night . . .*
> *And I knew that it was better to live out one's own*
> *absurdity than to die for that of others, whether for*
> *Ras's or Jack's.*

(See QUOTATIONS*, p. 72)*

The narrator learns that Ras is inciting the violent destruction, and he realizes that the Brotherhood had planned the race riots all along, deliberately ceding power to Ras and allowing Harlem to fall into mass chaos. He becomes caught up in one rioter's plans to burn down a tenement building and runs from the burning building, only to realize he has left his briefcase inside. He risks the flames to retrieve it. He wants to put on his Rinehart costume, which is in his briefcase, but the sunglasses have broken. Continuing to run through the chaos, he comes to a looted building where bodies appear to hang lynched from the ceiling. In fact, the bodies are mannequins. He then encounters a spear-wielding Ras, dressed in the costume of an Abyssinian chieftain and riding a black horse. Ras calls for his followers to lynch the narrator as a traitor to the black people and to hang him among the mannequins. The narrator tries to explain that the black community, by turning against itself now, by burning and looting its own homes and stores, is only falling into the trap that the Brotherhood has set. But Ras yells for the narrator's death, and the narrator runs away. He escapes only to encounter two police officers in the street, who ask to see the contents of his briefcase. He runs and falls through an open manhole into a coal cellar. The police mock him and put the manhole cover back in place, trapping him underground.

In order to provide himself with light, the narrator burns the items in his briefcase one by one. These include his high school diploma and Clifton's doll. He finds the slip of paper on which Jack had written his new Brotherhood name and also comes across the anonymous threatening letter. As the papers burn to ashes, he realizes that the handwriting on both is identical. He sleeps and dreams of Jack, Emerson, Bledsoe, Norton, and Ras. The men mock him, castrate him, and declare that they have stripped him of his illusions. He wakes with their cries of anguish and fury ringing in his ears. He decides to stay underground and affirms, "The end was in the beginning."

SUMMARY: EPILOGUE

> *I have . . . been called one thing and then another while no one really wished to hear what I called myself. . . . I am an invisible man.*

(See QUOTATIONS, *p. 73*)

The narrator concludes his story, saying that he has told all of the important parts. "I'm an invisible man and it placed me in a hole—or showed me the hole I was in, if you will—and I reluctantly accepted the fact." He doesn't know whether his decision to stay underground has placed him in the rear of social activism or in the avant-garde. He decides to leave that question to people such as Jack while attempting to study the lessons of his own life.

He realizes that he accrued the most hate to himself in the moments when he tried to speak and act with the most honesty. Similarly, he never received more love than at the moments when he worked to affirm the misguided beliefs of others. He has decided to escape this dilemma by becoming invisible. He has found a secret room in a closed-off section of a basement. His own mind agitates him, stirs him to thought. He keeps thinking of his grandfather's advice to "agree 'em to death," noting that his attempt to say "yes" to the Brotherhood ended only in a farce. The narrator then begins to reconsider the meaning of his grandfather's words, wondering if his grandfather's "yes" was meant as an affirmation of the principles on which the country was built rather than of the men who corrupted its name. Perhaps by saying "yes," his grandfather meant to take responsibility for society's evils and thus transcend them.

The narrator states that he doesn't covet Jack's power, Rinehart's freedom, or even the freedom not to run. He has stayed in his hole in order to figure out exactly what he wants. Hiding underground, he has learned that he is invisible but not blind. He ponders the tendency of the outside world to make all people conform to a pattern. He decides that life is to be lived, not controlled, and that our human fate is to become "one, and yet many."

The narrator then recounts an incident that occurred on the subway: an elderly white man was wandering around the platform, seeming lost but embarrassed to ask for directions. It was

Mr. Norton. He finally approached the narrator and asked how to get to Centre Street. The narrator asked if Mr. Norton knew who he was, mentioning the Golden Day. Norton asked why he should recognize the narrator, and the narrator replied, "Because I'm your destiny . . . I made you." He asked Norton if he wasn't ashamed. Norton clearly believed that the narrator was mad, and the narrator laughed hysterically as Norton boarded the train.

The narrator wonders why he has bothered to write his story down, as he feels that the effort has failed. He has found that the writing process has not helped him to cast his anger out into the world, as he had hoped, but rather has served to diminish his bitterness. The narrator declares the end of his hibernation: he must shake off his old skin and come up for breath. Even the disembodied voice of an invisible man, he asserts, has social responsibility.

Analysis: Chapters 24–Epilogue

The episode with Sybil may serve to comment on the similar positions of white women and black men in society. As in Chapter 19, Ellison portrays a white woman as a neglected wife, not at all interested in politics. Like the woman in Chapter 19, Sybil relates to the narrator as an abstraction, an object to be used for one's own purposes, and he relates to her in much the same manner. Perhaps Sybil, having been objectified and denied many potential outlets to define herself as an individual, faces some of the same frustrations that the narrator has faced; she may try to alleviate this frustration by treating another person as she has been treated. The narrator's motives in this scene appear more directed—he specifically wants information on the Brotherhood—but perhaps he subconsciously feels the same need as the white woman to assert his power over someone.

Although the narrator has sensed that the Brotherhood kept secrets from him, he now recognizes that he has fallen victim to a hugely tragic deception. In following the white leaders of the Brotherhood and in remaining loyal despite his suspicions of the organization's racism, the narrator has felt that he has betrayed his black heritage. Now, however, he realizes that his allegiance to the Brotherhood has rendered him a traitor twice: not only did he betray his heritage by working for a racist group, but he also played an active role in the group's plan to destroy New York's black community. The lynched mannequins function as a grotesque metaphor for the Brotherhood's figurative lynching of the narrator; indeed, Ras's threat to lynch and hang him amid these mannequins evidences how the Brotherhood has tried to destroy him.

The text emphasizes the narrator's exploited status in the scene in which he becomes covered with bird droppings. Bird droppings appear earlier in the novel as well, covering the statue of the Founder of the narrator's college. Much as people like Dr. Bledsoe manipulate the Founder as an abstract symbol and not as a person, the narrator has been used as an abstract symbol by the Brotherhood. He and the Founder have suffered the same fate: both have been used as a means to dupe others into blind allegiance to an ideology.

The narrator's encounter with Ras in Chapter 25 testifies to the influence of the French existentialists on *Invisible Man*. Faced with the prospect of death, the narrator decides in a climactic moment that he would rather live out his own "absurdity" than die for someone else's. The concept of absurdity plays a central role in the existentialist school of thought, which portrays the world as "absurd"—that is, full of labor and effort while lacking inherent value or meaning. The positive program of existentialism calls for the individual to affirm his or her own worth and sense of meaning despite the absurdity of the universe. The narrator's realization of the world's absurdity prepares him to write his memoirs and eventually cast off his invisibility at the end of the Epilogue. This realization may also allow him to see his grandfather's deathbed advice in a new light, noting its aspects of affirmation. In the Epilogue, thus, the narrator ponders whether to "agree 'em to death" might mean not to engage in a farcical masquerade all of one's life but rather to say "yes" to the world, to try to make it a better place, and, in so doing, to rise above those who would divide and destroy. If we consider *Invisible Man* as an existential bildungsroman, this moment with Ras constitutes the culmination of the narrator's growth throughout the novel and the moment of existential breakthrough.

This section instances Ellison's extraordinary gift for incorporating symbolism into the action of his story. The narrator's briefcase figures as a rich metaphor during the riot. First given to him by the white men in the "battle royal" scene in Chapter 1, the briefcase and its contents have come to symbolize the manipulation that the narrator has suffered: the Sambo doll and its invisible strings, the remains of Mary's coin bank, the piece of paper bearing his Brotherhood title, and the anonymous letter warning him not to assert himself too strongly. The briefcase and its contents represent moments from the novel in which others have tried to define his identity. Therefore, even as the narrator flees through the streets, he cannot find safety or freedom. He carries these items not only as literal but also as figurative baggage: as he runs, he drags along a burden of stereotypes and prejudices. He makes a metaphorical break with his past when he burns all of the items in the briefcase.

At the end of the novel, the narrator's story has come full circle: the novel begins and ends with his underground life. The story's cyclical nature, along with the narrator's claim that his time of hibernation is over, implies that the narrator stands poised for a kind of rebirth. During his period of hibernation, the narrator has studied his experiences and has sought to define the meaning of experience for himself, to define his own identity without interference from others. He rejects the idea that a single ideology can constitute an entire way of being; a perfect society created according to a single ideology would necessary limit the complexity of each individual, for each individual constitutes a multitude of various strands, and a society of individuals must necessarily mirror this diversity. As the novel draws to a close, the narrator remains bewildered regarding his own identity but determined to honor his individual complexity and his obligations to society as an individual.

IMPORTANT QUOTATIONS EXPLAINED

1. "I's big and black and I say 'Yes, suh' as loudly as any
    burrhead when it's convenient, but I'm still the king down
    here. . . . The only ones I even pretend to please are big
    white folk, and even those I control more than they control
    me. . . . That's my life, telling white folk how to think
    about the things I know about. . . . It's a nasty deal and I
    don't always like it myself. . . . But I've made my place in
    it and I'll have every Negro in the country hanging on tree
    limbs by morning if it means staying where I am."

Dr. Bledsoe speaks these words to the narrator in Chapter 6 while
rebuking him for taking Mr. Norton to the less desirable parts of
campus. Bledsoe explains how playing the role of the subservient,
fawning black to powerful white men has enabled him to maintain
his own position of power and authority over the college. He mock-
ingly lapses into the dialect of uneducated Southern blacks, saying
"I's" instead of "I am." By playing the role of the "ignorant" black
man, Bledsoe has made himself nonthreatening to whites. Bledsoe
claims that by telling white men what they want to hear, he is able
to control what they think and thereby control them entirely. His
chilling final statement that he would rather see every black man in
America lynched than give up his place of authority evidences his
single-minded desire to maintain his power.

This quote contributes to the larger development of the novel in
several ways. First, it helps to explain Bledsoe's motivation for expelling
and betraying the narrator: the narrator has upset Bledsoe's strategy of
dissimulation and deception by giving Norton an uncensored peek
into the real lives of the area's blacks. More important, this speech
marks the first of the narrator's many moments of sudden disenchant-
ment in the novel. As a loyal, naïve adherent of the college's philosophy,
the narrator has always considered Bledsoe an admirable exponent of
black advancement; his sudden recognition of Bledsoe's power-hungry,
cynical hypocrisy comes as a devastating blow. This disillusionment
constitutes the first of many that the narrator suffers as the novel progresses, perhaps most notably at the hands of the Brotherhood.

2. "Our white is so white you can paint a chunka coal and
you'd have to crack it open with a sledge hammer to prove
it wasn't white clear through."

Lucius Brockway makes this boast to the narrator in Chapter 10.
The narrator has taken a job at the Liberty Paints plant, and Brockway is describing the properties of the "Optic White" paint whose
production he supervises. This quote exemplifies Ellison's use of
the Liberty Paints plant as a metaphor. In both Ellison's descriptions of the paint-mixing process and the relations between blacks
and whites in the company, the Liberty Paints plant emerges as
a symbol for the racial dynamics in American society. The main
property of Optic White, Brockway notes, is its ability to cover
up blackness; it can even whiten charcoal, which is often used to
make black marks upon—to spoil, in a sense—white paper. This
dynamic evokes the larger notion that the white power structure in
America, like the white paint, tries to subvert and smother black
identity. Prejudice forces black men and women to assimilate to
white culture, to mask their true thoughts and feelings in an effort
to gain acceptance and tolerance.

3. . . . the cast-iron figure of a very black, red-lipped and
wide-mouthed Negro . . . stared up at me from the floor,
his face an enormous grin, his single large black hand held
palm up before his chest. It was a bank, a piece of early
Americana, the kind of bank which, if a coin is placed in
the hand and a lever pressed upon the back, will raise its
arm and flip the coin into the grinning mouth.

This passage, from Chapter 15, describes the coin bank that the
narrator finds at Mary's just before he leaves to join the Brotherhood. Ellison uses the coin bank as a symbol for the harmful racial
stereotypes that the narrator has tried in vain to escape. The figure
represents the servile, obsequious slave, eager to provide self-effac-
ing amusement to white people, performing petlike tricks for them.
Moreover, the bank establishes a black man as an object, a decoration and a trivial toy to be played with and used by white people.
After the narrator leaves Mary's, he finds himself frustratingly unable to get rid of this insulting coin bank. The bank thus illustrates
another aspect of stereotype—its stubborn permanence, its horrible
tendency to follow a person throughout his or her life.

4. I looked at Ras on his horse and at their handful of guns
    and recognized the absurdity of the whole night and of the
    simple yet confoundingly complex arrangement of hope
    and desire, fear and hate, that had brought me here still
    running, and knowing now who I was and where I was
    and knowing too that I had no longer to run for or from
    the Jacks and the Emersons and the Bledsoes and Nortons,
    but only from their confusion, impatience, and refusal to
    recognize the beautiful absurdity of their American identity
    and mine. . . . And I knew that it was better to live out one's
    own absurdity than to die for that of others, whether for
    Ras's or Jack's.

The narrator experiences this moment of epiphany during his confrontation with Ras in Chapter 25. This scene represents a key moment in the narrator's existential breakthrough, as he realizes that
his own identity is the source of meaning in his life and that acting to fulfill the expectations of others can only prove destructive.
Ras's threatening to kill the narrator makes the narrator see the
world as meaningless and absurd and the complexity of American
life as equally absurd. (Ellison borrows the word "absurd" directly
from the work of the French existentialists, who characterized the
universe as such and claimed that the only meaning to be found
in existence is that with which the individual invests his own life.)
The only motivation to which the narrator can cling is an affirmation that his own absurdity is more important to him than Jack's or
Ras's. The action of hurling Ras's spear back at him demonstrates
the narrator's refusal to be subject any longer to others' visions and
demands—he finally commits himself fully to an attempt to assert
his true identity.

5. And my problem was that I always tried to go in everyone's
    way but my own. I have also been called one thing and
    then another while no one really wished to hear what I
    called myself. So after years of trying to adopt the opinions
    of others I finally rebelled. I am an invisible man.

In this quote from the Epilogue, the narrator very neatly encapsu-
lates the main source of his difficulties throughout the twenty-five
chapters of the novel. He has not been himself and has not lived
his own life but rather has allowed the complexity of his identity
to be limited by the social expectations and prejudices of others.
He has followed the ideology of the college and the ideology of the
Brotherhood without trusting or developing his own identity. Now,
however, he has realized that his own identity, both in its flexibility
and authenticity, is the key to freedom. Rinehart, a master of many
identities, first suggests to the narrator the limitless capacity for
variation within oneself. However, Rinehart ultimately proves an
unsatisfactory model for the narrator because Rinehart's life lacks
authenticity. The meaning of the narrator's assertion that he is "an
invisible man" has changed slightly since he made the same claim
at the beginning of the novel: whereas at the outset he means to call
attention to the fact that others cannot not see him, he now means to
call attention to the fact that his identity, his inner self, is real, even
if others cannot see it.

QUOTATIONS

KEY FACTS

FULL TITLE
Invisible Man

AUTHOR
Ralph Ellison

TYPE OF WORK
Novel

GENRE
Bildungsroman (a German word meaning novel of personal
"formation," or development), existentialist novel, African-
American fiction, novel of social protest

LANGUAGE
English

TIME AND PLACE WRITTEN
Late 1940s–1952, New York City

DATE OF FIRST PUBLICATION
1952, although the first chapter was published in the English
magazine Horizon five years earlier

PUBLISHER
Random House

NARRATOR
The narrator is an unnamed black man who writes the story as
a memoir of his life.

POINT OF VIEW
The narrator writes in the first person, emphasizing his
individual experience and his feelings about the events
portrayed.

TONE
Ellison often seems to join the narrator in his sentiments,
which range from bitterly cynical to willfully optimistic, from
anguish at his sufferings to respect for the lessons learned from
them. Ellison seems to write himself into the book through
the narrator. However, Ellison also frequently portrays the

narrator as blind to the realities of race relations. He points out this blindness through other, more insightful characters (most notably the veteran) as well as through symbolic details.

TENSE

Past, with present-tense sections in the Prologue and Epilogue

SETTING (TIME)

The 1930s

SETTING (PLACE)

A black college in the South; New York City, especially Harlem

PROTAGONIST

The narrator

MAJOR CONFLICT

The narrator seeks to act according to the values and expectations of his immediate social group, but he finds himself continuously unable to reconcile his socially imposed role as a black man with his inner concept of identity, or even to understand his inner identity.

RISING ACTION

Dr. Bledsoe expels the narrator from college; the narrator gets into a fight over union politics with his black supervisor at the Liberty Paints plant and enters the plant hospital, where he experiences a kind of rebirth; the narrator stays with Mary, who fosters his sense of social responsibility; the narrator joins the Brotherhood.

CLIMAX

The narrator witnesses Clifton's racially motivated murder at the hands of white police officers; unable to get in touch with the Brotherhood, he organizes Clifton's funeral on his own initiative and rouses the black community's anger against the state of race relations; the Brotherhood rebukes him for his act of independence.

FALLING ACTION

Riots break out in Harlem, releasing the pent-up anger that has gathered since Clifton's funeral; the narrator encounters Ras, who calls for him to be lynched; running from Ras and the police, the narrator falls into a manhole and remains underground in "hibernation."

THEMES

Racism as an obstacle to individual identity; the limitations of ideology; the danger of fighting stereotype with stereotype

MOTIFS

Blindness; invisibility; jazz and blues music; masks and subterfuge; puppets and marionettes

SYMBOLS

The black Sambo doll; the coin bank; the Liberty Paints plant; the Brotherhood

FORESHADOWING

The narrator dreams that the scholarship given him by white community members in fact reads "Keep This Nigger-Boy Running." This prefigures the damaging influence on the narrator of his future college's lessons in ideology. When the narrator joins the Brotherhood, Brother Jack's mistress doubts aloud that the narrator is "black enough" to be the organization's black spokesperson. This hints at a latent racism within the Brotherhood, which will eventually end in the group's betrayal of the narrator.

Study Questions

1. *Compare and contrast the ideologies of the Brotherhood and the college. How does each ideology breed blindness and invisibility? What conflicts do they cause for the narrator?*

The college's ideology is based on the ideas of Booker T. Washington, who is represented by the figure of the Founder; through a near-religious devotion to the legend of the Founder's life, students at the college are taught to work hard and seek economic advancement while not clamoring for equal rights or equal treatment from whites. The college encourages students to reject black culture to the extent that it seems ignorant and rural, and to pattern their behavior on the white middle class. The Brotherhood adheres to an ideology based on that of American communist groups in the 1930s, a sort of authoritarian socialism that relies on a Marxist theory of history—which holds that those of lower social status must submit themselves to the unavoidable class struggles on the path to equality. The Brotherhood thus prizes clinical, scientific exposition over the sort of emotional appeal on behalf of the individual that the narrator makes after Tod Clifton's death.

The ideology of the college limits the narrator's identity in that it forces him to reject the black culture that shaped his early identity and forces him to accept a position of inherent inferiority to whites. The ideology of the Brotherhood limits the narrator's identity in that it requires blind adherence to the collective attitude of the organization and allows no room for individual thought, expression, or action—the very things that the narrator craves. By limiting the narrator's identity, these ideologies effectively render him invisible, as they force him to bury his real self beneath the roles that those around him require him to play.

2. *Who is Rinehart? What does he represent? What does he mean to the narrator?*

Rinehart is a mystery and a source of deep ambiguity in *Invisible Man*. He never appears in the novel, and the narrator only learns of his existence when other people mistake him for Rinehart while he is in disguise. Rinehart seems to be all things to all people—pimp, bookie, and preacher, among other things. Ultimately, Rinehart is an extremely surreal figure of Ellison's creation, designed not to be realistic or believable but rather unsettling and confusing. Rinehart represents a protean conception of identity—the idea that a person's identity can change completely depending on where one is and with whom one interacts, an extreme version of the narrator's conundrum throughout the novel. At first, the narrator feels that Rinehart's adaptability enables a kind of freedom, but he quickly realizes that Rinehart's formlessness also represents a complete loss of individual selfhood. In the end, the liquidity of Rinehart's identity is one of the forces that compel the narrator to discover his own more solid identity.

STUDY QUESTIONS

3.   *What is the role of treachery in the novel? Who betrays whom? How does treachery relate to the motifs of blindness and invisibility?*

The two major betrayals in the novel are the narrator's betrayals at the hands of the college (in the figure of Dr. Bledsoe) and the Brotherhood (in the figure of Brother Jack). Bledsoe poses as a figure representing the advancement of black Americans through education. In reality, however, he deliberately subordinates himself to whites and says that he would see every black man in America lynched before giving up his power. That he sends the narrator away with letters of supposed recommendation that, in reality, explicitly criticize the narrator demonstrates his objectionable desire to suppress black identity. The members of the Brotherhood betray the narrator in a number of insidious ways, ranging from curtailing his individuality to turning their backs on the plight of the poor blacks in Harlem. Jack, specifically, betrays the narrator by posing as a compassionate and helpful friend while secretly harboring racist prejudice against him and using him as a tool for the advancement of the Brotherhood's ends.

This sort of treachery generally contributes to the novel's creation of a bewildering, malevolent world in which an unexpected blow can come at any time, reinforcing the novel's characterization of the social effects of racial prejudice. Treachery also reinforces the ideas of blindness and invisibility, because any betrayal is essentially a sign that the betrayer willfully refuses to see his victim. Additionally, the novel's betrayals function through deceit and secrecy—for the most part, they are invisible, and the narrator is blind to them until it is too late.

How to Write
Literary Analysis

The Literary Essay: A Step-by-Step Guide

When you read for pleasure, your only goal is enjoyment. You might find yourself reading to get caught up in an exciting story, to learn about an interesting time or place, or just to pass time. Maybe you're looking for inspiration, guidance, or a reflection of your own life. There are as many different, valid ways of reading a book as there are books in the world.

When you read a work of literature in an English class, however, you're being asked to read in a special way: you're being asked to perform *literary analysis*. To analyze something means to break it down into smaller parts and then examine how those parts work, both individually and together. Literary analysis involves examining all the parts of a novel, play, short story, or poem—elements such as character, setting, tone, and imagery—and thinking about how the author uses those elements to create certain effects.

A literary essay isn't a book review: you're not being asked whether or not you liked a book or whether you'd recommend it to another reader. A literary essay also isn't like the kind of book report you wrote when you were younger, where your teacher wanted you to summarize the book's action. A high school- or college-level literary essay asks, "How does this piece of literature actually work?" "How does it do what it does?" and, "Why might the author have made the choices he or she did?"

The Seven Steps
No one is born knowing how to analyze literature; it's a skill you learn and a process you can master. As you gain more practice with this kind of thinking and writing, you'll be able to craft a method that works best for you. But until then, here are seven basic steps to writing a well-constructed literary essay:

1. *Ask questions*
2. *Collect evidence*
3. *Construct a thesis*

83

4. Develop and organize arguments
5. Write the introduction
6. Write the body paragraphs
7. Write the conclusion

---

1. ASK QUESTIONS

When you're assigned a literary essay in class, your teacher will often provide you with a list of writing prompts. Lucky you! Now all you have to do is choose one. Do yourself a favor and pick a topic that interests you. You'll have a much better (not to mention easier) time if you start off with something you enjoy thinking about. If you are asked to come up with a topic by yourself, though, you might start to feel a little panicked. Maybe you have too many ideas—or none at all. Don't worry. Take a deep breath and start by asking yourself these questions:

- **What struck you?** Did a particular image, line, or scene linger in your mind for a long time? If it fascinated you, chances are you can draw on it to write a fascinating essay.

- **What confused you?** Maybe you were surprised to see a character act in a certain way, or maybe you didn't understand why the book ended the way it did. Confusing moments in a work of literature are like a loose thread in a sweater: if you pull on it, you can unravel the entire thing. Ask yourself why the author chose to write about that character or scene the way he or she did and you might tap into some important insights about the work as a whole.

- **Did you notice any patterns?** Is there a phrase that the main character uses constantly or an image that repeats throughout the book? If you can figure out how that pattern weaves through the work and what the significance of that pattern is, you've almost got your entire essay mapped out.

- **Did you notice any contradictions or ironies?** Great works of literature are complex; great literary essays recognize and explain those complexities. Maybe the title (*Happy Days*) totally disagrees with the book's subject matter (hungry orphans dying in the woods). Maybe the main character acts one way around his family and a completely different way around his friends and associates. If you can find a way to explain a work's contradictory elements, you've got the seeds of a great essay.

At this point, you don't need to know exactly what you're going to say about your topic; you just need a place to begin your exploration. You can help direct your reading and brainstorming by formulating your topic as a *question*, which you'll then try to answer in your essay. The best questions invite critical debates and discussions, not just a rehashing of the summary. Remember, you're looking for something you can *prove or argue* based on evidence you find in the text. Finally, remember to keep the scope of your question in mind: is this a topic you can adequately address within the word or page limit you've been given? Conversely, is this a topic big enough to fill the required length?

Good Questions

> "Are Romeo and Juliet's parents responsible for the deaths of their children?"
> "Why do pigs keep showing up in Lord of the Flies?"
> "Are Dr. Frankenstein and his monster alike? How?"

Bad Questions

> "What happens to Scout in To Kill a Mockingbird?"
> "What do the other characters in Julius Caesar think about Caesar?"
> "How does Hester Prynne in The Scarlet Letter remind me of my sister?"

---

2. Collect Evidence

Once you know what question you want to answer, it's time to scour the book for things that will help you answer the question. Don't worry if you don't know what you want to say yet—right now you're just collecting ideas and material and letting it all percolate. Keep track of passages, symbols, images, or scenes that deal with your topic. Eventually, you'll start making connections between these examples and your thesis will emerge.

Here's a brief summary of the various parts that compose each and every work of literature. These are the elements that you will analyze in your essay, and which you will offer as evidence to support your arguments. For more on the parts of literary works, see the Glossary of Literary Terms at the end of this section.

ELEMENTS OF STORY   These are the *what*s of the work—what happens, where it happens, and to whom it happens.

- **Plot:** All of the events and actions of the work.

- **Character:** The people who act and are acted upon in a literary work. The main character of a work is known as the *protagonist.*

- **Conflict:** The central tension in the work. In most cases, the protagonist wants something, while opposing forces (antagonists) hinder the protagonist's progress.

- **Setting:** When and where the work takes place. Elements of setting include location, time period, time of day, weather, social atmosphere, and economic conditions.

- **Narrator:** The person telling the story. The narrator may straightforwardly report what happens, convey the subjective opinions and perceptions of one or more characters, or provide commentary and opinion in his or her own voice.

- **Themes:** The main idea or message of the work—usually an abstract idea about people, society, or life in general. A work may have many themes, which may be in tension with one another.

ELEMENTS OF STYLE   These are the *how*s—how the characters speak, how the story is constructed, and how language is used throughout the work.

- **Structure and organization:** How the parts of the work are assembled. Some novels are narrated in a linear, chronological fashion, while others skip around in time. Some plays follow a traditional three- or five-act structure, while others are a series of loosely connected scenes. Some authors deliberately leave gaps in their works, leaving readers to puzzle out the missing information. A work's structure and organization can tell you a lot about the kind of message it wants to convey.

- **Point of view:** The perspective from which a story is told. In *first-person point of view,* the narrator involves him or herself in the story. ("I went to the store"; "We watched in horror as the bird slammed into the window.") A first-person narrator is usually the protagonist of the work, but not always. In *third-person point of view,* the narrator does not participate in the story. A third-person narrator may closely follow a specific character, recounting that individual character's thoughts or experiences, or it may be what we call an *omniscient* narrator. Omniscient narrators see and know all: they can witness any event in any time or place and are privy to the inner thoughts and feelings of all characters. Remember that the narrator and the author are not the same thing!

- **Diction:** Word choice. Whether a character uses dry, clinical language or flowery prose with lots of exclamation points can tell you a lot about his or her attitude and personality.

- **Syntax:** Word order and sentence construction. Syntax is a crucial part of establishing an author's narrative voice. Ernest Hemingway, for example, is known for writing in very short, straightforward sentences, while James Joyce characteristically wrote in long, incredibly complicated lines.

- **Tone:** The mood or feeling of the text. Diction and syntax often contribute to the tone of a work. A novel written in short, clipped sentences that use small, simple words might feel brusque, cold, or matter-of-fact.

- **Imagery:** Language that appeals to the senses, representing things that can be seen, smelled, heard, tasted, or touched.

- **Figurative language:** Language that is not meant to be interpreted literally. The most common types of figurative language are *metaphors* and *similes,* which compare two unlike things in order to suggest a similarity between them—for example, "All the world's a stage," or "The moon is like a ball of green cheese." (Metaphors say one thing *is* another thing; similes claim that one thing is *like* another thing.)

---

3. CONSTRUCT A THESIS

When you've examined all the evidence you've collected and know how you want to answer the question, it's time to write your thesis statement. A *thesis* is a claim about a work of literature that needs to be supported by evidence and arguments. The thesis statement is the heart of the literary essay, and the bulk of your paper will be spent trying to prove this claim. A good thesis will be:

- **Arguable.** "*The Great Gatsby* describes New York society in the 1920s" isn't a thesis—it's a fact.

- **Provable through textual evidence.** "*Hamlet* is a confusing but ultimately very well-written play" is a weak thesis because it offers the writer's personal opinion about the book. Yes, it's arguable, but it's not a claim that can be proved or supported with examples taken from the play itself.

- **Surprising.** "Both George and Lenny change a great deal in *Of Mice and Men*" is a weak thesis because it's obvious. A really strong thesis will argue for a reading of the text that is not immediately apparent.

- **Specific.** "Dr. Frankenstein's monster tells us a lot about the human condition" is *almost* a really great thesis statement, but it's still too vague. What does the writer mean by "a lot"? *How* does the monster tell us so much about the human condition?

GOOD THESIS STATEMENTS

Question: In *Romeo and Juliet*, which is more powerful in shaping the lovers' story: fate or foolishness?

Thesis: "Though Shakespeare defines Romeo and Juliet as 'star-crossed lovers' and images of stars and planets appear throughout the play, a closer examination of that celestial imagery reveals that the stars are merely witnesses to the characters' foolish activities and not the causes themselves."

Question: How does the bell jar function as a symbol in Sylvia Plath's *The Bell Jar*?

Thesis: "A bell jar is a bell-shaped glass that has three basic uses: to hold a specimen for observation, to contain gases, and to maintain a vacuum. The bell jar appears in each of these capacities in *The Bell Jar*, Plath's semi-autobiographical novel, and each appearances marks a different stage in Esther's mental breakdown."

Question: Would Piggy in *The Lord of the Flies* make a good island leader if he were given the chance?

Thesis: "Though the intelligent, rational, and innovative Piggy has the mental characteristics of a good leader, he ultimately lacks the social skills necessary to be an effective one. Golding emphasizes this point by giving Piggy a foil in the charismatic Jack, whose magnetic personality allows him to capture and wield power effectively, if not always wisely."

4. DEVELOP AND ORGANIZE ARGUMENTS

The reasons and examples that support your thesis will form the middle paragraphs of your essay. Since you can't really write your thesis statement until you know how you'll structure your argument, you'll probably end up working on steps 3 and 4 at the same time.

There's no single method of argumentation that will work in every context. One essay prompt might ask you to compare and contrast two characters, while another asks you to trace an image through a given work of literature. These questions require different kinds of answers and therefore different kinds of arguments. Below, we'll discuss three common kinds of essay prompts and some strategies for constructing a solid, well-argued case.

TYPES OF LITERARY ESSAYS

- **Compare and contrast**

  Compare and contrast the characters of Huck and Jim in THE ADVENTURES OF HUCKLEBERRY FINN.

  Chances are you've written this kind of essay before. In an academic literary context, you'll organize your arguments the same way you would in any other class. You can either go *subject by subject* or *point by point*. In the former, you'll discuss one character first and then the second. In the latter, you'll choose several traits (attitude toward life, social status, images and metaphors associated with the character) and devote a paragraph to each. You may want to use a mix of these two approaches—for example, you may want to spend a paragraph a piece broadly sketching Huck's and Jim's personalities before transitioning into a paragraph or two that describes a few key points of comparison. This can be a highly effective strategy if you want to make a counterintuitive argument—that, despite seeming to be totally different, the two objects being compared are actually similar in a very important way (or vice versa). Remember that your essay should reveal something fresh or unexpected about the text, so think beyond the obvious parallels and differences.

- **Trace**

  Choose an image—for example, birds, knives, or eyes—and trace that image throughout MACBETH.

  Sounds pretty easy, right? All you need to do is read the play, underline every appearance of a knife in *Macbeth,* and then list them in your essay in the order they appear, right? Well, not exactly. Your teacher doesn't want a simple catalog of examples. He or she wants to see you make *connections* between those examples—that's the difference between summarizing and analyzing. In the *Macbeth* example above, think about the different contexts in which knives appear in the play and to what effect. In *Macbeth,* there are real knives and imagined knives; knives that kill and knives that simply threaten. Categorize and classify your examples to give them some order. Finally, always keep the overall effect in mind. After you choose and analyze your examples, you should come to some greater understanding about the work, as well as your chosen image, symbol, or phrase's role in developing the major themes and stylistic strategies of that work.

- **Debate**

    Is the society depicted in 1984 *good for its citizens?*

In this kind of essay, you're being asked to debate a moral, ethical, or aesthetic issue regarding the work. You might be asked to judge a character or group of characters (*Is Caesar responsible for his own demise?*) or the work itself (*Is* JANE EYRE *a feminist novel?*). For this kind of essay, there are two important points to keep in mind. First, don't simply base your arguments on your personal feelings and reactions. Every literary essay expects you to read and analyze the work, so search for evidence in the text. What do characters in *1984* have to say about the government of Oceania? What images does Orwell use that might give you a hint about his attitude toward the government? As in any debate, you also need to make sure that you define all the necessary terms before you begin to argue your case. What does it mean to be a "good" society? What makes a novel "feminist"? You should define your terms right up front, in the first paragraph after your introduction.

Second, remember that strong literary essays make contrary and surprising arguments. Try to think outside the box. In the *1984* example above, it seems like the obvious answer would be no, the totalitarian society depicted in Orwell's novel is *not* good for its citizens. But can you think of any arguments for the opposite side? Even if your final assertion is that the novel depicts a cruel, repressive, and therefore harmful society, acknowledging and responding to the counterargument will strengthen your overall case.

5. WRITE THE INTRODUCTION

Your introduction sets up the entire essay. It's where you present your topic and articulate the particular issues and questions you'll be addressing. It's also where you, as the writer, introduce yourself to your readers. A persuasive literary essay immediately establishes its writer as a knowledgeable, authoritative figure.

An introduction can vary in length depending on the overall length of the essay, but in a traditional five-paragraph essay it should be no longer than one paragraph. However long it is, your introduction needs to:

- **Provide any necessary context.** Your introduction should situate the reader and let him or her know what to expect. What book are you discussing? Which characters? What topic will you be addressing?

- **Answer the "So what?" question.** Why is this topic important, and why is your particular position on the topic noteworthy? Ideally, your introduction should pique the reader's interest by suggesting how your argument is surprising or otherwise counterintuitive. Literary essays make unexpected connections and reveal less-than-obvious truths.

- **Present your thesis.** This usually happens at or very near the end of your introduction.

- **Indicate the shape of the essay to come.** Your reader should finish reading your introduction with a good sense of the scope of your essay as well as the path you'll take toward proving your thesis. You don't need to spell out every step, but you do need to suggest the organizational pattern you'll be using.

Your introduction should not:

- **Be vague.** Beware of the two killer words in literary analysis: *interesting* and *important*. Of course the work, question, or example is interesting and important—that's why you're writing about it!

- **Open with any grandiose assertions.** Many student readers think that beginning their essays with a flamboyant statement such as, "Since the dawn of time, writers have been fascinated with the topic of free will," makes them sound important and commanding. You know what? It actually sounds pretty amateurish.

- **Wildly praise the work.** Another typical mistake student writers make is extolling the work or author. Your teacher doesn't need to be told that "Shakespeare is perhaps the greatest writer in the English language." You can mention a work's reputation in passing—by referring to *The Adventures of Huckleberry Finn* as "Mark Twain's enduring classic," for example—but don't make a point of bringing it up unless that reputation is key to your argument.

- **Go off-topic.** Keep your introduction streamlined and to the point. Don't feel the need to throw in all kinds of bells and whistles in order to impress your reader—just get to the point as quickly as you can, without skimping on any of the required steps.

---

6. WRITE THE BODY PARAGRAPHS

Once you've written your introduction, you'll take the arguments you developed in step 4 and turn them into your body paragraphs. The organization of this middle section of your essay will largely be determined by the argumentative strategy you use, but no matter how you arrange your thoughts, your body paragraphs need to do the following:

- **Begin with a strong topic sentence.** Topic sentences are like signs on a highway: they tell the reader where they are and where they're going. A good topic sentence not only alerts readers to what issue will be discussed in the following paragraph but also gives them a sense of what argument will be made *about* that issue. "Rumor and gossip play an important role in *The Crucible*" isn't a strong topic sentence because it doesn't tell us very much. "The community's constant gossiping creates an environment that allows false accusations to flourish" is a much stronger topic sentence— it not only tells us *what* the paragraph will discuss (gossip) but *how* the paragraph will discuss the topic (by showing how gossip creates a set of conditions that leads to the play's climactic action).

- **Fully and completely develop a single thought.** Don't skip around in your paragraph or try to stuff in too much material. Body paragraphs are like bricks: each individual one needs to be strong and sturdy or the entire structure will collapse. Make sure you have really proven your point before moving on to the next one.

- **Use transitions effectively.** Good literary essay writers know that each paragraph must be clearly and strongly linked to the material around it. Think of each paragraph as a response to the one that precedes it. Use transition words and phrases such as *however, similarly, on the contrary, therefore,* and *furthermore* to indicate what kind of response you're making.

---

7. Write the Conclusion

Just as you used the introduction to ground your readers in the topic before providing your thesis, you'll use the conclusion to quickly summarize the specifics learned thus far and then hint at the broader implications of your topic. A good conclusion will:

- **Do more than simply restate the thesis.** If your thesis argued that *The Catcher in the Rye* can be read as a Christian allegory, don't simply end your essay by saying, "And that is why *The Catcher in the Rye* can be read as a Christian allegory." If you've constructed your arguments well, this kind of statement will just be redundant.

- **Synthesize the arguments, not summarize them.** Similarly, don't repeat the details of your body paragraphs in your conclusion. The reader has already read your essay, and chances are it's not so long that they've forgotten all your points by now.

- **Revisit the "So what?" question.** In your introduction, you made a case for why your topic and position are important. You should close your essay with the same sort of gesture. What do your readers know now that they didn't know before? How will that knowledge help them better appreciate or understand the work overall?

- **Move from the specific to the general.** Your essay has most likely treated a very specific element of the work—a single character, a small set of images, or a particular passage. In your conclusion, try to show how this narrow discussion has wider implications for the work overall. If your essay on *To Kill a Mockingbird* focused on the character of Boo Radley, for example, you might want to include a bit in your conclusion about how he fits into the novel's larger message about childhood, innocence, or family life.

- **Stay relevant.** Your conclusion should suggest new directions of thought, but it shouldn't be treated as an opportunity to pad your essay with all the extra, interesting ideas you came up with during your brainstorming sessions but couldn't fit into the essay proper. Don't attempt to stuff in unrelated queries or too many abstract thoughts.

- **Avoid making overblown closing statements.** A conclusion should open up your highly specific, focused discussion, but it should do so without drawing a sweeping lesson about life or human nature. Making such observations may be part of the point of reading, but it's almost always a mistake in essays, where these observations tend to sound overly dramatic or simply silly.

A+ Essay Checklist

Congratulations! If you've followed all the steps we've outlined above, you should have a solid literary essay to show for all your efforts. What if you've got your sights set on an A+? To write the kind of superlative essay that will be rewarded with a perfect grade, keep the following rubric in mind. These are the qualities that teachers expect to see in a truly A+ essay. How does yours stack up?

- ✓ Demonstrates a thorough understanding of the book
- ✓ Presents an original, compelling argument
- ✓ Thoughtfully analyzes the text's formal elements
- ✓ Uses appropriate and insightful examples
- ✓ Structures ideas in a logical and progressive order
- ✓ Demonstrates a mastery of sentence construction, transitions, grammar, spelling, and word choice

Suggested Essay Topics

1. How does the narrator's briefcase encapsulate his history? Consider the contents of the briefcase. Consider also the dream that he has about the briefcase after the "battle royal." How does the briefcase relate to the narrator's position as a fugitive? What might the briefcase tell us about the narrator's identity?

2. What does the extended metaphor of dolls (the Sambo doll, for example) mean? What do they say about the power of racial stereotypes?

3. What does the veteran mean when he tells the narrator, "Be your own father"? What is the role of fathers or father figures in the novel? Think about the narrator's accusation that Jack wants to be the "great white father" and the description of the Founder's statue.

4. How does Ellison use irony to underline the difference between surface appearances and what lies beneath them? Consider Ellison's literary treatment of Reverend Barbee as one example. What are other examples?

5. What is the relationship between individual identity and community identity? Is it possible to remain true to both? Must the two always conflict? How does the narrator fail or succeed to assert his individuality amid communities such as the college, the Brotherhood, and Harlem?

A+ STUDENT ESSAY

> Choose one character in the novel and analyze his or her
> particular form of blindness.

Blindness—of both the literal and figurative varieties—figures heavily in *Invisible Man*. Blindness symbolizes the deliberate avoidance of truth, and in the novel it has the power to remake the world according to its vision (or lack thereof). The narrator, for example, claims that he has turned invisible because other people refuse to see him. Racial prejudice is the most pernicious form of blindness in Ellison's novel, but it is not the only one. Mr. Norton, a wealthy, white trustee of the narrator's college, cannot or will not see the true nature of his black beneficiaries' lives. But even more damaging, the book suggests, is his inability to acknowledge the true nature of his own self.

Like many white characters in the novel, Norton is blind to the realities of black people's lives. However, his form of prejudice is more covert than others, as he outwardly presents himself as a great supporter of black causes. Despite his generous financial donations to the college, Norton is unable—or unwilling—to see the abstract "Negroes" about whom he theorizes as real, individual human beings with specific thoughts and feelings. Tellingly, Norton never asks the narrator's name as they drive around campus together, even as he maintains that the two of them share the same destiny. In all his years as a supporter of the school, he has never been off campus grounds. In order to sustain an idealized image of black people, Norton remains willfully ignorant of the real conditions of their lives, sacrificing the particular and the individual for the comforting illusion of false generalities. When Norton does come face to face with the reality of life outside campus grounds, through his exposure to Trueblood and the Golden Day tavern, he suffers a heart attack, an apparent sign of his inability to handle the truth.

If his figurative blindness prevents Norton from properly seeing his black beneficiaries, it also prevents him from properly seeing himself. With his suave and genteel manner, Norton is to all appearances a benevolent trustee—and so he believes himself to be. Yet while he claims that his altruism empowers the students, in reality, the opposite is true. Norton takes pride in his work with the college not because of a selfless dedication to social causes, but because it gives him the power to direct and control the students' lives. Norton states that the college students are "bound to a great dream and to a beautiful monument." Ellison's use of the word "bound" here draws a parallel—perhaps unconscious on Norton's part—between the trustee-student relationship and the slaveholder-slave relationship. The fates of the students are "bound" to the wills of the trustees just as the lives of slaves were bound, physically and literally, to the whims of their master.

Ellison shows how people can be blind to the motives behind their ideals and their actions; in Norton's interaction with Trueblood, he shows how people can be blind to their own desires, as well. Norton's fascinated response to Trueblood's tale of incest suggests that beneath his deceptively innocent face—"pink like St. Nicholas"—Norton shares Trueblood's perverse instincts. Norton expresses fervid devotion for his own daughter, deliriously describing her beauty in poetic terms. He confesses to the narrator that he "could never believe her to be [his] own flesh and blood"—a seeming expression of humility, but also a hint that Norton might be able to deny his own fatherhood and therefore feel justified in expressing sexual feelings for his daughter. Norton expresses a bizarre empathy with Trueblood. Though repulsed by his actions, he also seems to somehow covet the man's incestuous relationship with his daughter. He insists on having a personal audience with Trueblood to hear the intimate details of his story, and then voyeuristically hangs onto his every word. The novel suggests that Norton achieves a certain vicarious enjoyment from Trueblood's tale, imaginatively participating in a forbidden act he also desires to commit. "You did and are unharmed!" he accuses him, with something like envy mixed in with his indignation. Norton's encounter with Trueblood reveals that beneath the white skin and rosy cheeks of this powerful, wealthy man, his "true blood" runs the same color as that of the poor, uneducated black man.

The veteran at the Golden Day tavern removes both Norton's and the narrator's figurative blindfolds. He shows the two men the similarities between them, declaring that, just as Norton wishes to believe himself a morally respectable, influential humanitarian, the narrator wishes to sustain the illusion that the college offers him an ideal education and the freedom to determine his own fate and identity. By refusing to acknowledge his own naiveté, the narrator is just as responsible for his own enslavement as his captor is. The fog of false idealism causes both the narrator's and Norton's blindness. While idealism may be necessary to instigate any kind of social change, *Invisible Man* asserts that, unless adopted with a degree of critical distance, it may also be responsible for the forms of prejudice it seeks to alleviate.

GLOSSARY OF LITERARY TERMS

ANTAGONIST

The entity that acts to frustrate the goals of the *protagonist*. The antagonist is usually another *character* but may also be a non-human force.

ANTIHERO / ANTIHEROINE

A *protagonist* who is not admirable or who challenges notions of what should be considered admirable.

CHARACTER

A person, animal, or any other thing with a personality that appears in a *narrative*.

CLIMAX

The moment of greatest intensity in a text or the major turning point in the *plot*.

CONFLICT

The central struggle that moves the *plot* forward. The conflict can be the *protagonist*'s struggle against fate, nature, society, or another person.

FIRST-PERSON POINT OF VIEW

A literary style in which the *narrator* tells the story from his or her own *point of view* and refers to himself or herself as "I." The narrator may be an active participant in the story or just an observer.

HERO / HEROINE

The principal *character* in a literary work or *narrative*.

IMAGERY

Language that brings to mind sense-impressions, representing things that can be seen, smelled, heard, tasted, or touched.

MOTIF

A recurring idea, structure, contrast, or device that develops or informs the major *themes* of a work of literature.

NARRATIVE

A story.

LITERARY ANALYSIS

NARRATOR

The person (sometimes a *character*) who tells a story; the *voice* assumed by the writer. The narrator and the author of the work of literature are not the same person.

PLOT

The arrangement of the events in a story, including the sequence in which they are told, the relative emphasis they are given, and the causal connections between events.

POINT OF VIEW

The *perspective* that a *narrative* takes toward the events it describes.

PROTAGONIST

The main *character* around whom the story revolves.

SETTING

The location of a *narrative* in time and space. Setting creates mood or atmosphere.

SUBPLOT

A secondary *plot* that is of less importance to the overall story but may serve as a point of contrast or comparison to the main plot.

SYMBOL

An object, *character,* figure, or color that is used to represent an abstract idea or concept. Unlike an *emblem,* a symbol may have different meanings in different contexts.

SYNTAX

The way the words in a piece of writing are put together to form lines, phrases, or clauses; the basic structure of a piece of writing.

THEME

A fundamental and universal idea explored in a literary work.

TONE

The author's attitude toward the subject or *characters* of a story or poem or toward the reader.

VOICE

An author's individual way of using language to reflect his or her own personality and attitudes. An author communicates voice through *tone, diction,* and *syntax.*

LITERARY ANALYSIS

A Note on Plagiarism

Plagiarism—presenting someone else's work as your own—rears its ugly head in many forms. Many students know that copying text without citing it is unacceptable. But some don't realize that even if you're not quoting directly, but instead are paraphrasing or summarizing, *it is plagiarism* unless you cite the source.

Here are the most common forms of plagiarism:

- Using an author's phrases, sentences, or paragraphs without citing the source
- Paraphrasing an author's ideas without citing the source
- Passing off another student's work as your own

How do you steer clear of plagiarism? You should *always* acknowledge all words and ideas that aren't your own by using quotation marks around verbatim text or citations like footnotes and endnotes to note another writer's ideas. For more information on how to give credit when credit is due, ask your teacher for guidance or visit www.sparknotes.com.

REVIEW & RESOURCES

QUIZ

1. What color is Brother Jack's hair?

    A. Red
    B. Brown
    C. Blond
    D. Gray

2. From what company does the narrator steal electricity?

    A. The Standardized Light & Power Co.
    B. Pacific Gas
    C. Monopolated Light & Power
    D. The New York Energy Authority

3. What jazz recording does the narrator describe in the Prologue?

    A. "Dippermouth Blues," by King Oliver
    B. "(What Did I Do to Be So) Black and Blue," by Louis Armstrong
    C. "I Thought I Heard Buddy Bolden Say," by Jelly Roll Morton
    D. "Barnyard Blues," by the Original Dixieland Jazz Band

4. In Chapter 1, what do the white men give the narrator after his speech?

    A. A hundred-dollar bill
    B. A new jacket
    C. A job
    D. A scholarship to college

5.   Of what sin is Jim Trueblood guilty?

    A.   Incest
    B.   Murder
    C.   Greed
    D.   Theft

6.   Why is the narrator expelled from college?

    A.   For cheating on his chemistry test
    B.   For punching a white man who taunted him
    C.   For his heavy marijuana use
    D.   For taking one of the founders to a nearby black tavern

7.   What does the narrator learn about Homer Barbee at Barbee's sermon?

    A.   That Barbee is deaf
    B.   That Barbee is blind
    C.   That Barbee was sterilized in an accident with lye
    D.   That Barbee has a club foot

8.   What is Ellison's attitude toward Booker T. Washington's philosophy of race relations?

    A.   He embraces it wholeheartedly.
    B.   He advocates it with some reservations.
    C.   He regards it with ambivalence.
    D.   He rejects it fiercely and repeatedly.

9.   What sort of accent does Ras the Exhorter have?

    A.   West Indian
    B.   Southern
    C.   Bostonian
    D.   French

10. Which of the following characters sells racially offensive dolls?

    A.   Brother Tarp
    B.   Brother Wrestrum
    C.   Brother Clifton
    D.   Brother Jack

11. What is the best-selling color at Liberty Paints?

    A. Regal Blue
    B. Optic White
    C. Blood Red
    D. Burnt Sienna

12. Which member of the Brotherhood offers the narrator a place in the organization?

    A. Brother Wrestrum
    B. Brother Tarp
    C. Brother Clifton
    D. Brother Jack

13. Where does the narrator give his first speech for the Brotherhood?

    A. In a boxing arena
    B. At the Harlem Meer
    C. At Madison Square Garden
    D. In front of a stable

14. Which woman allows the narrator to stay at her house her for free?

    A. Emma
    B. Sylvia
    C. Mary
    D. Juanita

15. When the narrator smashes a racially offensive coin bank, where does he stash the pieces?

    A. In a well
    B. In his briefcase
    C. In his safe-deposit box
    D. In an underground vault

16. What hinders the narrator and the other boys from collecting the money off of the rug after the "battle royal"?

   A. They are wearing blindfolds and thus cannot see.
   B. The coins and bills are glued to the rug.
   C. The rug is guarded by white men with guns.
   D. The rug is electrified.

17. For whom do people mistake the narrator when he dons dark glasses?

   A. "Wilman"
   B. "Rinehart"
   C. "Castlerock"
   D. "Johnson"

18. Who kills Tod Clifton?

   A. Ras
   B. The narrator
   C. The police
   D. The Brotherhood's henchmen

19. How many light bulbs does the narrator have burning in his underground room?

   A. 1,369
   B. 1,863
   C. 1,492
   D. 1,603

20. Who incites the riot in Harlem?

   A. The narrator
   B. Brother Wrestrum
   C. Brother Hambro
   D. Ras the Exhorter

21. Where was Ralph Ellison born?

   A. New York City, NY
   B. Mobile, AL
   C. Boston, MA
   D. Oklahoma City, OK

22. Which character has only one eye?

    A. The narrator's grandfather
    B. Brother Jack
    C. Sybil
    D. Mr. Norton

23. At the narrator's college, what covers the statue of the Founder?

    A. Sunlight
    B. Gold
    C. Bird droppings
    D. Tree sap

24. How does Dr. Bledsoe betray the narrator?

    A. By giving him letters of condemnation instead of recommendation
    B. By arranging to have him fired from Liberty Paints
    C. By seducing Alice
    D. By telling the Brotherhood about the narrator's eulogy for Clifton

25. What food makes the narrator think of the South?

    A. Peanut butter
    B. Okra
    C. Jambalaya
    D. Yams

SUGGESTIONS FOR FURTHER READING

BONE, ROBERT. "Ralph Ellison and the Uses of Imagination." In *A Casebook on Ralph Ellison's* INVISIBLE MAN, ed. Joseph F. Trimmer, pp. 203–224. New York: Thomas Y. Cromwell Company, 1972.

BUSBY, MARK. *Ralph Ellison.* New York: Twayne Publishers, 1991.

CALLAHAN, JOHN F., and ALBERT MURRAY, eds. *Trading Twelves: The Selected Correspondence of Ralph Ellison and Albert Murray.* New York: Modern Library, 2000.

ELLISON, RALPH. *Living with Music: Ralph Ellison's Jazz Writings.* Ed. Robert G. O'Meally. New York: Modern Library, 2000.

———. *Shadow and Act.* New York: Vintage Books, 1995.

NADEL, ALAN. *Invisible Criticism: Ralph Ellison and the American Canon.* Iowa City: University of Iowa Press, 1988.

O'MEALLY, ROBERT, ed. New Essays on INVISIBLE MAN. New York: Cambridge University Press, 1988.

TRACY, STEVEN C. *A Historical Guide to Ralph Ellison.* Oxford, UK: Oxford University Press, 2004.

REVIEW & RESOURCES